NEW CHINA, FRIEND OR FOE?

Harvest   Hsia Feng

The above illustration and those at the end of various chapters are of paper cut-out window decorations, a traditional peasant art very popular in the new China.

NEW CHINA

Friend or Foe?

By ALUN FALCONER
Foreword by
JOSEPH NEEDHAM
ScD, FRS

Foreign Languages Press

First published by the Naldrett Press Ltd., London, UK, 1950.

Home Page:
   http://www.flp.com.cn
E-mail Addresses:
   info@flp.com.cn
   sales@flp.com.cn

ISBN 7-119-03540-1

Foreign Languages Press, Beijing, 2004

Published by Foreign Languages Press

24 Baiwanzhuang Road, Beijing 100037, China

Printed in the People's Republic of China

PREFACE

Huang Hua

It is a great honor for me to write a preface for the new, PFS (China Society for People's Friendship Studies) 50-book series under the general title of *Light on China.* All these books were written in English by journalistic and other eyewitnesses of the events described. I have read many of them over the seven decades since my student days at Yenching University. With some of the outstanding authors in this series I have ties of personal friendship, mutual regard, and warm memories dating from before the Chinese people's Liberation in 1949.

Looking back and forward, I am convinced that China is pursuing the right course in building a strong and prosperous country in a rapidly changing world with its complex and sometimes volatile developments.

The books in this series cover a span of some 150 years, from the mid 19th to the early 21st century. The numerous events in China, the sufferings and struggles of the Chinese people, their history and culture, and their dreams and aspirations were written by foreign observers animated by the spirit of friendship, equality and cooperation. Owing to copyright matters and other difficulties, not all eligible books have as yet been included.

The founder of the first Chinese republic, Dr. Sun Yat-sen wrote in his Testament in 1925, "For forty years I have devoted myself to the cause of the people's revolution with but one end in view: the elevation of China to a position of freedom and equality among the nations. My experiences during those forty years have convinced me that to attain this goal we must bring about an awakening of our own people and ally ourselves in common struggle with those people of the world who regard us as equals."

Chairman Mao Zedong declared, at the triumphal founding of the People's Republic in 1949, "The Chinese people have stood up." Today, having passed its 53rd anniversary, we see the vast forward strides that have been taken, and note that many more remain to be made.

Many foreign observers have traced and reported the real historical movement of modern China, that is: from humiliation — through struggle — to victory. Seeking understanding and friendship with the Chinese people, their insight and perspective were in basic harmony with the real developments in China. But there have been others who viewed China and the Chinese people through glasses tinted by hostile prejudice or ignorance and have invariably made irrelevant observations that could not stand the test of time. This needs to be better understood by young people and students, at home and abroad. The PFS series *Light on China* can help them gain an overview of what went before, is happening now, and will emerge in the future.

Young students in China can additionally benefit from these works by seeing how foreign journalists and authors use fluent English to record and present historical, philosophical, and socio-political issues and choices in China. For millions of students in China, English has become a compulsory second language. These texts will also have many-sided usefulness in conveying knowledge of our country to other peoples.

Students abroad, on their part, may be helped by the example of warm, direct accounts and impressions of China presented by their elders in the language that most readily reaches them.

Above all, this timely and needed series should help build bridges of friendship and mutual understanding. Good books long out of print will be brought back to strengthen the edifice.

My hearty thanks and congratulations go first to ex-Premier Zhu Rongji, who has been an effective supporter of this new, PFS series. They go to all engaged in this worthy project, the Foreign Languages Press, our China Society for People's Friendship Studies, and others who have given their efforts and cooperation.

Chairman Mao Zedong has written: "So many deeds cry out to be done, and always urgently. The world rolls on, time presses. Ten thousand years are too long. Seize the day, seize the hour."

The hour has come for making these books available to young people in China and abroad whose destiny is to build a better world together. Let this series add a small brick to that structure.

Beijing, Autumn 2003

CONTENTS

FOREWORD

By JOSEPH NEEDHAM

ScD, FRS

Formerly Director of the Sino British Science Co-operation Office, Chungking.

IT is a pleasure indeed to have the opportunity of commending the book of Alun Falconer to the wide range of readers which it will assuredly have. Nothing could be more timely than the appearance of a book which will have the effect of awakening sympathy in the English-speaking world for the people of China as they press forward along the new path which they have decisively chosen. If one had to select one single phrase from any of the author's chapters as a keynote of the book, I should be tempted to refer to what he says on page 52, namely, that the Chinese communists are strong not because they have curtailed democracy in China, but because they are immensely extending it. And to this might be added the point which comes out clearly from page 54, that however Marxist the social and economic theories of the party of Chairman Mao Tse-Tung may be, the successes so far attained, and those which will be reached in the future, can only be the result of a profound adaptation of these theories to the concrete conditions of Chinese society.

Though Mr Falconer writes as a practical journalist rather than an academic scholar, it is most noteworthy that he sees the necessity of an attempt to sketch the historical background of Chinese civilization in its social and economic aspects. It cannot be emphasized too much that the growth of Chinese civilization took place along lines quite different from those with which we are familiar in our own part of the world, Europe. Everyone knows of the achievements of Græco-Roman civilization, its law and literature, its art and science; everyone knows of its limitations due to reliance on slave-labour. Familiar, too, is the way in which it gave place to the feudalism of what we call the Middle Ages, and how at the Renaissance, the Reformation, and the rise of capitalism, this feudal culture was overthrown and superseded by a fundamentally mercantile culture. From the outset, Europe was marked by the co-existence of city-states and maritime navigation. Nor do we need to be reminded of the gradual growth of socialist ideas within the bosom of capitalist society, until the great changes of our own time took place. But what is not generally recognized is that China (and to a large extent the whole of East and South Asia) had a very different history. When, about the second century BC, the classical phase of Chinese feudalism began to give place to a new form of social life, there was no development of mercantilism and capitalism, but the formation of a new type of society unknown in the West, which may be called 'bureaucratic feudalism'. Possibly this had existed before, in Egypt and in Babylonia; at any rate it was a state of society in which the intermediate and minor feudal lords ceased to exist, and the Emperor governed by means of a vast (and mainly non-hereditary) civil service—the 'Mandarinate'. In such a society the idea of the independent city-state of mercantile adventurers was unknown, and the predominantly agrarian and non-maritime character of the Asian land-mass inhibited that development of autonomous merchants and sea-captains so characteristic of Europe.

For many years past the Asian peoples have recognized that there was urgent necessity for the modernization and industrialization of their countries, since science and technology in the modern sense, with all the power over Nature which they have brought to mankind, and all that they imply for the raising of the standard of life of the peoples, were not spontaneously developed by the Asian civilizations. But while it was agreed on all hands that this development of the natural resources of Asia must come about, it was not at all certain how it would happen. Must China, for example, pass through all the weary stages of capitalist development which had occurred in Western Europe, the era of the 'dark satanic mills' of which William Blake spoke, the industrial horrors of the time of the Factory Acts, and the grinding wretchedness of the newly formed industrial proletariat which populated the great manufacturing cities of our own country in their early days? This question was for long a very real one to me. I knew well men and women who had worked in the Factory Inspection Bureau of the Shanghai Municipality, and the stories which they had to tell of the girls literally sold to, and imprisoned in, the textile mills on the Japanese model. Far to the west, in Yunnan province, I knew the conditions in the tin mines, where naked and stunted children, in the full grip of multiple forms of malnutrition, and with an average life-expectancy of a dozen years, burrowed through clefts in the rock impassable for adults, in bringing the ore to the surface. In Kansu province to the north I myself saw the same things in the primitive coal-mines there. This was primitive, of course, but it could all have passed over with little or no amelioration into the state of affairs which would have existed in a China fully undergoing capitalist exploitation.* But the alternative was that China might be able to pass, by some mighty leap forward, from mediæval bureaucratic feudalism, not to capitalism, but to socialism, or at least to a system of social leadership which would guarantee the attainment of socialism at the earliest possible time. Fundamentally this is the decision which the Chinese people have taken in winning their civil war against the Kuomintang (a party once revolutionary, but for many years past no longer so). It is only in the light of this background that their decision can be understood. Here in the present book its details will be found.

The very deep differences between the historical development of European countries on the one hand and of China and other Asian countries on the other would also be well worth emphasizing if only for the purpose of making it clear

---

* Credit must be given where it is due. During the war the Chinese National Resources Commission, a government corporation controlling and operating numerous mines and factories, had a very enlightened workers' welfare policy, as I personally found on many occasions. But under a fully capitalist China it is extremely unlikely that these beginnings would have persisted and developed.

that what suits one part of the world may not suit another. In welcoming the great social revolution which has just taken place in China, and is now being consolidated there, no Englishman is called upon to change his own political convictions, whether Conservative or Labour. The urgent need for the strengthening of friendly ties between Britain and China is too obvious. Commercial relations have always been close, and everything should be done to see that trade continues on a scale even greater than that of the past. The Chinese will recognize and appreciate all possible technical advice and assistance from Britain, for they will assuredly not be able to get all that they need from the countries of Eastern Europe, though their relations with them will naturally be closer henceforward than formerly. Every effort should be made to encourage intellectual contacts, and to promote exchanges with the Chinese universities and technical schools—and in this connection a tribute should be paid to the British Council, which through all the difficult times of the last two or three years, has never wavered in its liberal policy of giving travelling fellowships for Chinese students, and of exchanging scientific and humanistic literature and the like.

Mr Falconer refers (on page 8) to the higher technology of the West in modern times, which, after its introduction to China, had such a profound effect on the indigenous culture. It should, however, be more generally realized than it is, that this Western 'superiority' is comparatively modern, a thing only of the past three hundred years. Before that, for fourteen centuries, there was a steady flow of discoveries and inventions westward, which were taken over by Europeans often without knowledge of where they had come from. Certain examples of these inventions are well known, such as paper, printing, gunpowder, and the magnetic compass, but a great many more could be cited. It might indeed be said that while the typical civilization of China was much less effective in technological invention than that of post-Renaissance Europe, it was much more so than that of feudal and ancient Europe. The reasons for these differences are still obscure, and constitute fascinating problems for the historian. But socially speaking, the important thing was that, by a series of historical causes, that previously unimaginable power over Nature which springs from modern mathematized natural science, and which Francis Bacon was one of the first to visualize, came initially into the possession of Europeans and not of the Asian peoples. The 'dominance' psychology which this developed in Europe (and in that extension of European culture, North America) led to the whole story of colonial imperialism, and found one of its most pithy expressions in Belloc's famous lines:

> *'... For we have got*
> *The Maxim Gun, and they have not.'*

Today, however, we are witnessing a revolt against this attitude on a scale of continental grandeur. Contemporary India, however distracted, and Indonesia, are examples of, at any rate, a temporary breathing-spell; China has achieved a decisive liberation; and the issue is joined in Indo-China, Malaya, Korea and elsewhere. It is not that the Asian peoples grudge recognition to the great geniuses, discoverers, scientists and scholars of the Occident; it is simply that they know now that they can produce scientists and engineers as competent and useful as those of any Western country, and that they do not see why the historical fact that modern science and technology first arose in the West gives Westerners any further title to colonial, semi-colonial, or commercial domination over Asian peoples. They wish, and intend, to govern themselves. And they would deny to Westerners any right to strategic occupation of Asian territories in the pursuance of their own quarrels. In all this there is nothing at all difficult to understand; the astonishing thing is that so few people in the West seem to have been able so far to realize what the Asian attitude is, and to respond to it with friendly comprehension.

Naturally no one, not even the writer of a foreword, can be expected to agree in all particulars with any given author. For my part, I should wish to question, on technical grounds, Mr Falconer's view (expressed on page 98) that the latinization (romanization) of the non-alphabetic Chinese language is either necessary or inevitable. But the points on which I should differ from him would not be important ones, and in no way affect my hearty recommendation of his excellent 'Tract for the Times'.

To
J.W.P., M.T.
P.T., and R.Y.

Prologue
STORM FROM THE NORTH

To: All foreign correspondents.

From: Chinese Government Information Office,

Shanghai Office, Broadway Mansions.

You are cordially invited to an informal tea-party given by Mr Fang Chih, Secretary-General of the Political Council of the Nanking-Shanghai-Hanchow Garrison Headquarters, at 11.00 hours tomorrow, May 24, 1949, at Apt. 40, 13th floor, Broadway Mansions.

R S V P.

THE tables were laid in the dining-room of Broadway Mansions looking down upon the sprawling city of Shanghai and the famous Bund. Beneath us, the streets were lined with Kuomintang flags. During the morning truckloads of employed demonstrators had paraded cheering and shouting slogans. Now a group of soldiers on guard at the edge of the Bund was blazing away at a small abandoned sampan drifting past down the Whangpoo.

Fang Chih arrived, a tall hawk-nosed man in grey, and the tea-party began. Below, the soldiers fired on desperately at the empty sampan.

'In order to deal the fatal blow at the Communist bandits, the Government made a decision to defend Shanghai to the last,' said Fang Chih. 'On this fourteenth day of the war of self-defence, General Tang En-po, with the highest determination, the groundwork completed, with happy and strong defence works, huge manpower, endless reserves of wealth, and the highest morale yet seen, has determined to defend the land and the people... Being thoroughly trained and well-balanced correspondents I would not doubt your duty to report this to the world...' When asked why there were flags in the streets, Fang Chih said gravely: 'It is a spontaneous celebration of our people over victory.'

At 5 p.m. that day, Fang Chih, with General Tang En-po, fled Shanghai in the last escaping aircraft,

Early the next morning advance squads of the Communist 3rd Field Army walked into the western suburbs and proceeded to take over the city together with some one hundred thousand demoralized Kuomintang troops. Shanghai, the largest city in China and in Asia, had fallen.

What could be reported to the world?

That, in China, the Communists had won.

That, if there had ever been any question about the outcome of the civil war, if there had ever been the slightest chance of reprieve for the Kuomintang armies, all doubts were now resolved. Shanghai and the greater part of China had passed into the hands of a new authority whose leadership was unchallenged, whose military strength was impressive, whose creed of 'New Democracy' would become law for the Chinese people—and they are one-fourth of humanity.

There is a Chinese proverb which can be translated: 'A bear coughs at the North Pole and the sands of the Sahara stir.' In Shanghai we had witnessed a storm coming from the north that could alter the climate of all Asia, and of the world. At least no one could now be fully equipped to make judgements about the state of things to come unless he understood the genesis of this storm, its strength, its nature and its course.

Why did the Communists Win?

There are two main trends of opinion on which the answers to this question are based.

One is represented by the letter of Secretary of State Dean Acheson accompanying his White Paper on China, which he addressed to President Truman at the end of July, 1949.

Mr Dean Acheson wrote that the Kuomintang, the party of Chiang Kai-shek, was a group of 'reactionaries who were indistinguishable from war-lords of the past' and whose Government as a result 'lost popular support'.

'The unfortunate but inescapable fact is that the ominous result of the civil war in China was beyond the control of the Government of the United States... It was the product of internal Chinese forces, forces which this country tried to influence but could not. A decision was arrived at within China, if only a decision by default.'

A decision by default!

The other trend of opinion is that expressed in a speech given in Peking on September 21, 1949, by Madame Sun Yat-sen:

'There is a momentum in this land today, The Chinese people are moving and they have the impact of revolution. There is a pulsation, a building, a new China! We have arrived at this historic position because of the leadership provided by the Chinese Communist Party. It is the only party which has the strength of the masses infused in its ranks. As a result, it is the surest guarantee that Sun Yat-sen's Three Principles—People's Nationalism, People's Democracy and People's Livelihood—will be successfully carried out.

'This has been proven in the countryside, where the Communist Party has given land to the tiller. It was on the backs of our peasants that the burden of the first phase of our revolution was carried ...'

The impact of revolution!

Here, then, are two conclusions drawn from the shattering events of 1949. Which is correct? Did the Communists win by default, or were they identified with a revolution which could not be contained?

Chapter One

THE LIBERATION OF SHANGHAI

O**N THE** twentieth of April, 1949, the Communists had crossed the Yangtse River line. In three days Nanking, the national capital, had fallen; and then Anking, capital of Anhwei province; and Wusih, Wuhu and Kiangyin. The fort commander at Kiangyin went over to the Communists with two regiments of garrison troops. A certain army commander was reported to have surrendered. Chiang Kai-shek had left for an undisclosed destination. The People's Liberation Army was encircling Shanghai.

I was at Lunghua Airport on April 28. There was an abnormal number of outgoing passengers that day. There were barriers across the roads and armed soldiers on the airfield. Telephone lines were jammed and the clerks in the customs section had no ink for their pens. They smiled helplessly as the disorderly pageant of voluntary refugees shouted for attention. At the head of the restless crowd stood a melancholy young man who wore three hats, one on top of the other. Behind him were the gentlemen in long grey gowns, fingers armoured with gold and precious stones; the foreign families with bulging suitcases; the pretty Chinese girls in high-heels, nylons and smart tailored suits. One distinguished foreign traveller held two prancing borzoi hounds on a leash. Both the master and the dogs were leaving.

I returned with difficulty to the centre of the city. The streets were an unbelievable confusion. Refugees and frightened peasants were pouring into Shanghai. People, carts, rickshaws, bicycles, pedicabs, trucks and every conceivable type of vehicle jammed the streets from side to side. But people could not escape from their fear. I watched a furious army officer kicking a pedicab coolie who was too slow in getting rid of his civilian passenger to make way for the officer and his baggage. At intersections the gendarmerie had set up sandbags and mounted light machine-guns.

On the pavements the confusion was doubled. Paper currency had become almost valueless and the ubiquitous Yellow Ox Gang was out in force trading silver dollars. And everywhere there were men and women begging the pedestrian to stop and buy lengths of silk, cotton, rubber-soled shoes, chairs, belts, pots and pans, suitcases, cigarettes and everything that was manufactured in the city. The sellers were factory workers, and their wares were goods they had made, given them instead of wages. Employers could no longer find enough paper money to go round. Hundreds of thousands of these amateur hawkers were on the streets of Shanghai.

And there was terror in the city. The red vans of the gendarmerie careered through the streets, sirens screaming. Soldiers had occupied all the universities and hundreds of students had been arrested. It was rumoured that Chang Lan, the Democratic League leader, was under arrest and detained in a local hospital.

Towards eleven each night the frantic streets suddenly emptied. Gates, windows, doors were barred. Curfew began, and an odd silence. Until, across the city, down the darkened streets, would come again the hideous sirens of the red police vans. Day and night.

At three o'clock on an afternoon in May a crowd began to gather outside the Foochow Road Police Station, the headquarters of the Kuomintang gendarmerie in Shanghai. A large black curtain shut off the central courtyard of the station from the street. Within the curtain, where I stood, there was an atmosphere of hysteria and terror. Nervous gendarmes and Kuomintang soldiers moved about, fingers on the trigger-guards of their loaded carbines and revolvers. At the back of the yard two chairs stood on a dais under a black flag decorated with the Kuomintang symbol.

Approaching from the street came the sirens of the red vans. The gendarmes sprang to life. The black curtain lifted, and a van roared into the yard.

The van door opened and the two condemned men were pushed out. Gendarmes seized them, twisted their arms behind their backs and thrust them forward, snarling at a photographer who happened to catch the scene.

Two high police officials had entered and occupied the chairs on the raised dais. We watched the two condemned men as they were thrust before them.

They were Meng Shih-heng and Shao Chien-kwei, both members of Marshal Li Chi-sen's Revolutionary Committee of the Kuomintang. They had been arrested three months before in Nanking and were accused of conspiring with Communists and organizing an attempted *coup d'état* against the Government. (Twenty years before Marshal Li Chi-sen had been a bitter anti-Communist and supporter of Chiang Kai-shek. But he had gradually disassociated himself from Chiang and become an advocate of coalition government, of unity between the Kuomintang and the Communist Party. In 1947 he had formed the Revolutionary Committee of the Kuomintang and won support for his policy of national unity among many honest members of the Kuomintang, such as the two men who now awaited sentence.)

From the high dais the senior police officer read out the formal notification of death sentences personally imposed by General Tang En-po on Meng Shih-heng and Shao Chien-kwei.

Lifting their heads they cried out their innocence, denying that they were traitors to China, insisting that they were martyrs to the true Kuomintang principles of Sun Yat-sen.

The senior officer wrote the orders for execution in red with a sweeping brush stroke across the fan-shaped placards on his desk. As the two condemned men were dragged to a waiting truck one of them cried in a shrill voice: 'Long live the Three People's Principles!'

The hysterical police clustered round them, motors roared, and the truck went out under the black curtain. As it went, we could hear the two men singing the song of the Kuomintang.

These two and another were taken to a street corner in Chapei and there shot—a warning to the people of Shanghai, and to all Chinese, that no principles on earth, not even the principles of the Kuomintang itself, could now be tolerated in Chiang Kai-shek's China.

The end was fast approaching. In Shanghai there was to be the mockery of the victory parade, the final convulsions, Fang Chih's peroration, and the anxious days while the fighting moved across the city.

Battle in Miniature

The Liberation Army did not walk into Shanghai entirely unopposed. For two days, detachments of Kuomintang soldiers fought a rearguard action along the line of Soochow Creek running east-west through the city. They entrenched themselves in the top floors of Broadway Mansions and other buildings. The Communist advance elements had come in from the south, and so the northern suburbs, including Hongkew, were in Kuomintang hands for two days.

It happened that I lived in Hongkew, in one of several apartments which opened onto a courtyard protected from the street by a large iron gate. But we felt extremely insecure, in fear of fire and looting. The old gateman, a survivor of other upheavals, had insisted that every family pay two silver dollars for the purchase of sheet-iron to reinforce the entrance,

It did protect us for several hours, but a small party of Kuomintang soldiers eventually forced their way in, They picked out the best apartments and they made themselves comfortable. And then, to my surprise, there began an intricate battle of wits and reason between the new guests and our Chinese neighbours that might have been a miniature of the whole Shanghai battle.

Our neighbours, who had rarely talked to one another before, formed themselves into a committee. They held a long discussion, and then turned upon the soldiers. These Kuomintang conscripts were a mixed bag. One was a red-cheeked boastful lad of sixteen; and two were old campaigners who rarely opened their mouths except to swallow, without comment, the food that our neighbours offered them. There was a medical officer who changed immediately into a borrowed suit of civvies, saying that he had been trying to get out of this army for over a year. And there was a thin glassy-eyed fanatic who threatened to bash in a servant's head with the butt of his rifle. In command was a sergeant: 'A reasonable, educated man,' said the merchant whose apartment he had commandeered.

The debate began. A post-office employee, a man whom we had scarcely noticed before, became the chief spokesman for the courtyard committee. 'You're done for,' he said quite bluntly to the soldiers. 'What's the use of dying without reason. Your fine general has saved his skin. That rotten egg! He dipped his hands into our pockets and cleared out.'

'All of us were given three silver dollars,' said the boastful youth. It was not a suggestion, but nevertheless our neighbours managed to slide small gifts into the soldiers' hands.

'Why go on fighting? Whom do you want to kill?'

The soldiers were silent. At last one of them shook his head: 'We're all Chinese,' he said. 'Why should we slaughter one another.'

Late that night the soldiers were called out on duty, but they returned in twos and threes early the next morning. The thin fanatic was no longer with them, and we let them in.

The debate continued. 'Look at these men,' one of our neighbours whispered. 'They have the best guns and plenty of ammunition. What have the Americans not given them? But they can't fight. They have no spirit.' He glanced at us. 'Heaven is on the side of the Communists.'

'The Communists won't harm you if you surrender.' The post-office employee was prodding them again. 'We're all brothers.'

Our merchant friend brought the soldiers rice. They were weakening. Finally the sergeant gave an order. When the Communists came he would surrender. Meanwhile, two soldiers should guard the gate and keep all others out.

That was how it happened. The next morning it was all over. The old gateman collected the pile of arms and torn uniforms that were heaped into the courtyard and carried them to the Communist soldiers posted in the street.

All Shanghai seemed to be in the streets gazing in awe at the strange men in mustard-yellow uniforms who were taking over with an air of swift, calm authority. Occasionally a group of workmen would stride by wearing white armbands and carrying rifles. A party of middle-school students came running along pasting up rough home-made posters: 'Welcome the People's Liberation Army: The Protectors of the People.' Some of our courtyard youngsters began to sing at the top of their voices the old anti-Japanese anthem, 'Chi Lai.'

Later some Communist soldiers came into our courtyard searching for prisoners and weapons. They were stern and methodical. Our *pao-chia* chief (the block's Kuomintang agent), who had spent the siege in hiding, suddenly appeared wearing his best blue gown and bearing an offering of cigarettes for the conquerors. The soldiers brushed him aside.

But, pressed by our neighbours' committee and the hordes of inquisitive children, they finally lost some of their stiff pride and stayed to talk and drink a glass of hot water. All else they refused—food, cigarettes and shelter.

That night in Shanghai they slept in the streets, huddled in doorways and on the ledges of shop-windows.

It was in those first twenty-four hours that the Communists secured their real victory.

The Second Army

But perhaps the most remarkable aspect of our two-day siege was that, although the city was split in half and there was continuous fighting, every essential public utility was kept running. While we were barricaded in our courtyard we could still telephone to our friends in the liberated southern suburbs. Water and electricity supplies were uninterrupted.

Nor was this by chance. One year before, at a national trade union conference held in Harbin (then in Communist hands), delegates from the illegal trade unions of Shanghai had given a guarantee that when the Liberation Army came to Shanghai all essential public utilities would be kept going whatever the circumstances. The employees of the Shanghai telephone companies, power companies and waterworks fulfilled their promise.

Not only workers, but also many of Shanghai's businessmen were prepared to accept with equanimity, even with tacit agreement, the entry of the Liberation Army. It was no 'fifth column' within Shanghai, but a whole second army of willing hands. Even among its own carefully groomed police the Kuomintang failed to hold authority. On the very eve of the fall of the city more than seventy policemen were summarily executed on the orders of their Kuomintang commander, Mao Sen.

The fact is that the Kuomintang left behind it a stench of death and corruption, while the Communists were accepted as liberators and acted with the discipline and *élan* of that role.

To Shanghai the change came with the force of the inevitable—overwhelming, decisive, absolute. Why was this? Because it was born out of all China's modern history.

The events in China today are incomprehensible unless we examine briefly the historical tensions and forces that generated them.

Chapter Two

A 'PERFECT GOVERNANCE'

T HERE was a civilization in China at the time of the Golden Age of Egypt, but, fortunately, to grasp the meaning of events in China in 1949 we need not go back much more than one hundred years, to the period of the Opium War (1841-42). Before this time Chinese society was feudal. Its political and economic conditions were essentially unaffected by any change of dynasty, any conflict within or invasion from without. That is, from the Chou dynasty and the Ch'in dynasty (about 1000-207 BC), there existed in China a relatively self-sufficient peasant economy controlled by a feudal landlord-gentry. The peasants were tied to the land by the social pressure of tradition, by armed threat and excessive debt; even the towns were strongholds of the gentry and their officialdom; the provinces were ruled by feudal governors, responsible to the imperial dynasties at the summit of the whole structure. There were stresses and strains on the surface of Chinese society, but the essential character remained.

It was not until the late eighteenth century that new forces, the rising pressure of the Industrial Revolution spreading irresistibly from Great Britain, Europe and America, set loose a chain of reactions within Chinese society that was to alter its whole nature.

In 1792 Lord Macartney presented a letter from the King of England to the Manchu Emperor, Chien Lung. The letter requested that permission be given for the opening of an Embassy in Peking, that Christian missionaries be allowed to preach in China, that ports other than Canton be thrown open to British merchantmen.

The English ambassador was treated with courtesy, but every one of the requests was refused. The elaborate reply sent to George III said that, as China possessed all things, China had no need of the products of England. 'Swaying the wide world, I have but one aim in view, namely, to maintain a perfect governance and to fulfil the duties of the State; strange and costly objects do not interest me. I (wrote the Emperor) have no use for your country's manufactures ...'

As we shall see, from the point of view of the stability of China's ancient economy and the continuation of the imperial order, this was not an ill-considered reply.

The Opium War

The Chinese resisted the growing pressure of British merchants and traders. In particular, they were opposed to the British opium merchants who sought to continue and expand their highly profitable trade with China in spite of restrictions imposed by the Manchu Government. This mounting clash of interests resulted in the Opium War, in which the British Government supported the policies of the merchants. The military resistance of the Manchus was overcome, and the fighting ended with the signing of the Treaty of Nanking in 1842.

The clauses of the Treaty of Nanking and the negotiations which followed had far-reaching consequences. Under the treaty, the Chinese Government agreed to pay to Britain the cost of British military expenditure in fighting the war. Thus was established the principle of indemnities. Further wars and defeats followed as all the great powers staked out their claims in China, legalizing their conquests by a series of 'unequal treaties'.

To ensure the payment of war indemnities, a customs service was set up in China under the control of Britain and other foreign powers. A low customs rate of 5 per cent was set on the value of all foreign goods imported. This meant that foreign manufactured products had easy access to China's markets; and that the Chinese were denied any form of import control which might have assisted the growth of native industry and help transform their economy to meet Western competition. At the same time revenue was drained from China, undermining the ability of the Government to finance national development, forcing it to levy heavier taxes upon its citizens, making it increasingly dependent on foreign loans. (Nor was this a temporary condition. In the five years from 1924 to 1928, for example, payment on foreign loans and indemnities absorbed 78 per cent of the net customs revenue in China.)

Further, a series of Treaty Ports were named in which Britain and other powers could establish settlements where foreigners might live under their own laws and jurisdiction. A separate treaty signed by Britain in 1843 established for all the powers the right to these privileges. This treaty included the 'most-favoured nation' clause, declaring that any foreign country should enjoy the rights won by all foreign countries in China. At one centre after another the powers established settlements and concessions where their nationals lived under the protection of troops, gunboats and exterritorial rights.

Thus, through the 'unequal treaties', China became a semi-colonial domain of all the great powers.

The Chain Reaction

We are not concerned here with the ethics of this development. Our problem is: what were its effects within China?

Comparisons are drawn with Japan. Japan, in the nineteenth century, was also penetrated by the forces of the Industrial Revolution. But Japan was able to maintain its sovereignty and to create its own industrial revolution in reply. In China, however, the changes and innovations introduced from the West were not allowed to develop according to China's own needs. For one hundred years the foreigner possessed superior military strength, higher industrial techniques and a tougher philosophy. His concessions in Canton, Shanghai, Tientsin and elsewhere were secure islands in troubled seas of revolution and counter-revolution. The modern industry that did develop gradually in China was concentrated within and near the foreign concessions. Though it benefited from a certain measure of protection, it was unrelated to sources of raw materials and to China's internal markets. It faced outwards, serving the interests of foreign investment.

With this, there was a 'distortion' of political power within China. As Owen Lattimore writes: 'Throughout this period the foreigners had only one device for ruling China which really counted: reliance on the Strong Man. The Strong Man, in practice, turned out always to be a man weak enough to accept orders and control from abroad, but strong enough to give orders and exercise control domestically.'* In the last fifty years of the nineteenth century (to which Lattimore refers) and beyond, the Manchus who fell in 1911, the war-lords Yuan Shih-kai, Wu Pei-fu and Chang Tso-lin who came after, and Chiang Kai-shek himself, all held power with semi-modern armies created to suppress domestic rebellion but unable to withstand assault from abroad.

It is not surprising that China became the stage for a succession of wars and revolutions: the Taiping Rebellion (1850-64), the Franco-Chinese War (1858-60), the Sino-Japanese War (1894-95), the Hundred Days of Reform (June 11-Sept. 16, 1898), the Boxer Rebellion (1900), the Revolution of 1911, the May 4 Movement (1919), the Nationalist Northern Expedition (1925-27), the Communist Agrarian Revolution, the War of Resistance against Japan, and the recent civil war.

Yet we have not come down to the central problem of modern China, the most significant effect of Western penetration, its intensification of the land problem.

The Peasant Problem: The Problem of Land

The last official census in China, issued by the Directorate of Statistics in Nanking in 1931, estimated that there were about 452 million people in

---

* The Making of Modern China. (*Allen & Unwin, London, 1945.*)

China, though by 1950 this figure had increased to about 475 million. Of this immense population, some 80 per cent derive their livelihood directly or indirectly from the land.

This agrarian population has not been homogeneous. There were the landlord-gentry who may have possessed holdings of upwards of 300 acres in the rich rice lands of the Yangtse valley and the south, or many thousands of acres in the *kaoliang* (millet) and wheat-growing areas of the north. There were the middle peasants, the independent farmers, fighting an endless battle to maintain their family holdings. And there was the great mass of poor and landless peasants whose average plot in north China has been estimated at five acres, in south China at 3.5 acres. Deep in debt, at the mercy of the landlords, plagued by flood and famine, bandits, soldiery and tax-collectors, they were, nonetheless, the strength and foundation of the old Chinese society.

In the last hundred years China's peasant population has steadily increased. Side by side with this, the customary division of land has continued—the father's land being divided among the sons, the son's land among the grandsons. These factors and ever-deepening poverty have driven the Chinese peasant northward into Manchuria, south into the lands of southeast Asia, overflowing into America, Australasia and the South Seas. It is poverty and the hunger for land that have forced the peasants from their homes.

The Chinese peasant does not sell or leave his land unless he is driven by desperation. The strongest traditions bind him to his earth, his village. It has been a characteristic of Chinese emigrants that they went abroad to work for their families, intending to return to their native land. In the past many even of China's city industrial workers have continued to be tied to their villages, entering the cities to supplement the family income for short periods only.

Yet at no time have the Chinese peasantry been able to make their living solely from the land. In some areas the number of peasants who have been able to support their families solely from the land has been set as low as 10 to 30 per cent. In the villages the people have always supplemented their earnings by craft industries, weaving, pottery, paper-making, basketry, and a multitude of small trades.

The most devastating effect of the entry of Western commerce and manu-factured products into China was their destruction of the traditional industry of the peasant village. In some cases local industries were wiped out. Few could compete against the products of Lancashire, Pennsylvania and modern Japan. The foreign goods were cheaper and their quality higher. The two eminent Chinese sociologists, Fei Hsiao-tung and Chang Chih-i, have written: 'Let us remind the reader of two fundamental facts in Chinese rural economy; the first is that traditional Chinese industry is diffuse among villages, and the second that the farmers depend upon it for subsistence. The industrial revolution in the West at last threatens the peasants in the Chinese villages in their capacity as industrialists. It is a hopeless struggle for the unorganized mass of petty owner-workers. However skilful they may be, they are fighting a losing battle against the machine. But they must keep on fighting, because otherwise they cannot live. The result is that China is gradually being reduced to an agrarian country, pure and simple; and an agrarian China is inevitably a starved China.

'The desperation of this situation is felt by every household where in-come is declining. Any stroke of misfortune will force the peasant owner to sell his land...'*

The peasant did sell his land. And that was not an end of his misfortune, but a beginning.

The days of 'perfect governance' were gone forever.

---

* Earthbound China. (*Routledge: Kegan Paul, London, 1949.*)

Chapter Three

THE NATIONAL REVOLUTION

IN HAWAII in 1894 a small group of Chinese students, young army officers and businessmen met to plan the overthrow of the Manchus, 'to unite the patriotic Chinese people, to cultivate the arts of wealth and power, for the purposes of reviving China.' They formed the *Shing Chung Wei*, the China Revival Society, and their leader was Sun Yat-sen.

During the previous fifty years the Manchu dynasty had brought China to the verge of ruin. China's sovereignty had been repeatedly encroached upon. Debts and indemnities had crippled the Government. It had begun to sell appointments in the civil service and the vast irrigation systems had fallen into disrepair. Merchants, scholars and peasants alike suffered under a despotic and corrupt regime. China was ready to listen to the prophets of a new life.

Sun Yat-sen was looked upon by some as an ineffectual visionary and by others as a dangerous rebel. But the man who was to become the Father of the Chinese Republic proved himself to be a statesman who bent his brilliant talents as an organizer, thinker and publicist to the achievement of a single objective: the unification of China under a Government strong enough to restore national sovereignty.

In the years until 1911 Sun Yat-sen was active in China and abroad,

14

hunted by his enemies and sometimes abandoned by his friends. His first adherents were young army officers, smarting under the shame of foreign occupation; student-scholars, denied their traditional place in society by the new practice of selling civilian appointments; merchants and struggling industrialists who could not compete against the privileged foreign trader. Not least among his supporters were the overseas Chinese, who hoped for a strong and independent China capable of defending their status.

The national revolutionary movement grew in scope and strength, and Sun Yat-sen's party (renamed the Kuomintang) took the lead. In 1911 a group of wealthy Chinese presented the Manchu Government with a project for the building of a railway. But the project was refused and the contract given to the consortium of four British, French, German and American banks within China. It was the last act of a Government which had already mortgaged its country to the foreigner and was so corrupt that no outside help could save it from the fury of its citizens. Revolt broke out in Hankow, where garrison troops rebelled, and quickly spread to Shanghai and Canton. An Assembly was created by the revolutionary elements, and Sun Yat-sen was recalled from abroad to become the Provisional President of the new Chinese Republic.

War-lords and a New Learning

The first Republic breached the walls of China's old society but it was powerless to advance. It had neither the military strength, the financial reserves, nor the organized mass support necessary to enforce its will. Against it were arrayed all the influences of the landlord-gentry dominating the bulk of China, many of the provincial governors, and, in the north, the political war-lord Yuan Shih-kai, who headed the remains of the Manchu Government. The foreign powers, realizing that the Manchus had lost all authority, were casting about for a new Strong Man who could keep the Republican forces in check and safeguard their concessions and investments. The more conservative elements in the Revolutionary National Assembly itself were wavering. They were anxious to consolidate their gains, to appease the powers and to secure new foreign loans. They, too, wanted a 'safe' leader.

Sun Yat-sen was rapidly isolated. In February, 1912, Yuan Shih-kai was asked to become President of the Republic, and Sun Yat-sen was forced to resign.

In 1914 Yuan Shih-kai reappointed himself President, with the right to nominate his successor, and ruled as a dictator. Republican Army and Kuomintang leaders were executed and driven into exile. Military governors were appointed side by side with the civil governors of the provinces. These men soon became war-lords, who appropriated most of the provincial revenue for themselves, appointed their own officials and created their own private provincial armies. All vestiges of national unity, civil government and discipline vanished. The last blow to the long-suffering peasantry was a decree ordering that all land tax must be paid in money and not in kind. Thus the peasants were driven deeper into debt and servitude to the landlords, and forced to turn increasingly to crops such as tobacco, wanted by the foreign commercial interests.

Instead of a restoration of sovereignty China now faced a period of the greatest humiliation in its modern history. The foreign debt was greater than ever before. Customs and salt revenues came under complete foreign control. Foreign advisers were appointed to key ministries in the Central Government. The railways, mines and the bulk of such modern industry as had developed were foreign operated and owned.

The greatest threat of all came from a rising, industrialized, militarist Japan. When the European Powers were embroiled in the Great War, Japanese imperialists enormously strengthened their economic, territorial and political concessions in China, and almost won complete control over the Central Government clique in Peking.

Paradoxically, during the first decades of the twentieth century, when the hatred against the foreigners in China reached new heights, the dispossessed intelligentsia were turned more sharply than ever against the ancient forms of Chinese culture and the ways of Chinese society, and reached out for Western learning. The works of Darwin, Adam Smith, the French Encyclopædists, the novels of Balzac, Gogol, Turgenev, Dickens, were all translated and became the textbooks of the New Learning. The most notable of modern China's cultural leaders, Lu Hsun, wrote: 'Whenever I read Chinese books I felt lugubrious, and it seemed to me that I formed no part of human existence; but whenever I picked up a foreign book—Indian books excepted—I felt galvanized into life and as though I had come into contact with human existence, and I also felt a *penchant* for doing and performing something.'

The young men of China were not turning to the West for escape but for inspiration. The Chinese culture they were rejecting was that of the discredited and impotent past, the Confucian analects and the rigid forms of classical literature. Hu Shih, Chin Tu-hsin and others led a strong literary reformation and began writing essays, stories and poetry in *pai-hua*, the spoken language of the common people.

It was a new and significant thing in China when the scholars began to consider themselves allies and spokesmen of the commoners, the *laopaihsing*. Kuo Mo-jo,* another notable scholar who studied medicine in Japan, wrote: 'What the devil is the use of studying medicine. You can kill parasites and germs, but how can you kill the loathsome social system which breeds them? It is comparatively easy to give the rich a dose of Epsom salts for their stomach troubles, but when you see the poor run down by motor-cars and armed soldiers slaughtering thousands of your fellow-countrymen ... What can a doctor do?'

The New Learning drew inspiration from Western culture, but faith in the intentions of the Western powers was badly shaken once again by the proclamation of the Treaty of Versailles, in which Shantung was handed over to the Japanese.

It was in an atmosphere of bitter antagonism to Japan and the foreign imperial powers that the Kuomintang, under the leadership of Sun Yat-sen, began to organize a second revolution in Canton.

---

* *Now chairman of the Committee of Cultural and Educational Affairs of the present Chinese Government.*

The May 4 Movement

On May 4, 1919, the students of Peking staged a mass demonstration calling for the resignation of pro-Japanese ministers. It was the first mass entry of China's students into political activity, and their action awoke an immediate and widespread response throughout the country. The Chinese delegates at Versailles refused to sign the Treaty. The May 4 Movement spread. Beginning as a demonstration of disapproval it became a tremendous force, uniting the intellectuals and common people of China in a demand for drastic reforms and the restoration of sovereignty. The forces were gathering for the next stage of the National Revolution.

China at this time was no longer isolated and without friends. The Russian Revolution in 1917 reverberated throughout Asia. The collapse of great empires in the 1914-18 war and the emergence of a new revolutionary power pledged to support the nationalist movement among colonial peoples had an incalculable effect on the people of China and the East. One of the first acts of the Soviet Government was to annul the Tsar's 'unequal treaties' with China.

This and subsequent actions of the Soviet Government had a profound influence on Sun Yat-sen and on the policy of the Kuomintang. Sun Yat-sen is reported to have said: 'The republic is my child. It is in danger of drowning. I am trying to keep it afloat and we are being swept down the river. I call for help to England and America. They stand on the bank and jeer at me. There comes a Russian straw. Drowning, I clutch at it. England and America, on the bank, shout at me on no account to clutch that Russian straw. But do they help me? No.'*

After several failures the Kuomintang again succeeded in establishing a Government in Canton under the leadership of Sun Yat-sen and its new military chief, Chiang Kai-shek. Although it could claim authority over little more than the province of Kwangtung, the policies of the Kuomintang were now clearer and its support much broader. The first

---

* The Chinese Puzzle, *by Arthur Ransome (Allen & Unwin, London, 1927).*

National Congress of the party, convened in Canton in 1924, declared that: 'Only if the peasants and the workers join in can the national revolutionary movement be victorious.' It allowed into its ranks members of the Chinese Communist Party, which had been founded in 1921. Mao Tsetung him self attended the 1924 conference and later became head of the propaganda department of the Kuomintang and candidate for the Central Committee. A Communist, Lin Pai-ch'u, became the head of the peasant department, and another Communist, T'an P'ing-shan, head of the workers' department.

The Canton Govermnent decided upon the creation of a modern volunteer army. At first attempts were made to recruit army officers from Canada and the United States, but their Governments refused them permission to travel to China. Again Sun Yat-sen turned to Soviet Russia. Many Soviet army officers went to Canton as individual volunteers and a few air-force instructors came from the German Weimar Republic. Chiang Kai-shek was sent to study in Russia.

Clarifying the policies of the new national revolution, Sun Yat-sen gave a series of lectures to his followers in Canton on the subjects of 'Nationalism', 'Democracy' and 'People's Livelihood'. These famous lectures, though incomplete at the time of Sun Yat-sen's death in 1925, furnished the Kuomintang and its allies with broad and popular slogans into which the Chinese people could read all their aspirations.

Canton to Nanking

In June, 1926, the Canton Government launched its famous Northern Expedition to destroy the war-lords and unify China. The revolutionary Government had a popular programme and a disciplined and reasonably equipped army that was superior to any that the war-lords of central China could muster. Moreover, the way was paved by revolutionary agitators who went out ahead of Chiang Kai-shek's battalions organizing peasant unions, disarming the *mintuan* (landlord militia), and calling upon the workers of the cities to rebel. Industrial workers in Shanghai, formed into armed detachments under the direction of Chou En-lai*, seized the Chinese quarters of the city in March, 1927, in preparation for the arrival of the Nationalist armies advancing steadily from the south. The old society was being rent apart at the seams.

But, at this stage, there began a second struggle within the national revolutionary movement itself, a struggle motivated by sectional interests, political rivalry, personal ambitions and international diplomacy. The main feature of this struggle was an open break between the Kuomintang and the Chinese Communist Party. The climax came with the establishment of a new Central Government in Nanking in 1928. Communists were driven from every position of influence and hunted down. Diplomatic relations with the Soviet Union were severed. Those whom Sun Yat-sen had united were now committed to a future of bitter civil war.

China was left with a relatively strong Government in Nanking that tried to unify China by agreement with the provincial war-lords rather than by popular revolution, and to extend national sovereignty by compromising with the Western powers. The Central Government in Nanking was completely in the hands of the right-wing majority of the Kuomintang. The supreme authority in the Kuomintang was its commander-in-chief, General Chiang Kaishek.

Yet Chiang Kai-shek was too close to Sun Yat-sen to appear merely as another war-lord or dictator. Instead he appeared as the inheritor of the will of Sun Yat-sen, dedicated to the famous *San Min Chu I*, Sun Yat-sen's Three People's Principles of Nationalism, Democracy and People's Livelihood. In fact, it was essential for him to do so. At the height of the national revolution the Three People's Principles had become the embodiment of the needs and expectations of the Chinese people. On the fulfilment of these principles in accordance with China's needs Chiang Kai-shek was either to advance or fall.

China Under Chiang

Talk of People's Livelihood in China has no meaning unless it is con-

---

* *Now Premier of the Central People's Government.*

cerned with the problem of the land, the indebtedness of the peasantry and the destruction of village industry.

The 1926 programme of the Kuomintang promised '25 per cent reduction of rent on agricultural lands', and Chiang Kai-shek often declared that the policy of the Nanking Government was to restrict large holdings with the ultimate aim that every peasant should possess his own land. At one stage an Act was passed fixing land rent at $37^1/_2$ per cent of yearly production. Attempts were made to foster credit co-operatives and so weaken the hold of village usurers. But the Acts, plans and promises remained largely on paper. If they did anything to mitigate the desperate situation of the peasant, other factors outweighed them and worsened the whole situation.

In 1920 China had begun to import rice! This trend was never reversed. And China's silk industry withered under increasing Japanese competition. Taxes increased by leaps and bounds, in some districts by 300 per cent.* The provincial war-lords made even further demands on their citizenry, and Chiang's central armies, maintained and expanded under civil war conditions, were a heavy drain on the national resources.

All the trends that began in the last years of the Manchus, and were intensified under Yuan Shih-kai, continued to force the peasants to sell and divide their land. Some writers state that more than half the peasants became tenant farmers and that more and more land passed into the hands of the landlords and usurers, until estates of over 3,000 acres were no longer the exception even in south China. In the early 'thirties, 95 per cent of the population were earning at rates below the subsistence level (less than £14.10s. a year).**

The Nanking Government did take some steps towards strengthening the country's economy by expanding China's transport system, building roads and railways, and establishing airlines. But no serious efforts were made to face the task of industrializing China, fundamentally the only policy that

---

* China Struggles for Unity, *Pringle*. (*Penguin Books, London, 1939.*)
** Facing Labour Issues in China. *Lowe Chuan-hua* (*Shanghai, 1933.*)

could prevent the transformation of the nation into a poverty-stricken 'agrarian country, pure and simple'.

Chinese-owned cotton spinning mills had numbered 77 in 1925: in 1930 there were only 81. In the same time foreign-owned mills increased in number from 37 to 46. Even as late as 1937, only one quarter of the industrial capital invested in China was Chinese. Actually the wealthy Chinese tended to invest their capital in land rather than industry, being attracted by the high rents and rapid returns on credit. Industry was a sickly orphan and no one was ready to pay for its schooling.

Was it that the Nanking Government did not realize that without economic sovereignty there could be no political sovereignty? Or was it that the very interests who gave allegiance to the Nanking Government were opposed to any economic revolution?

It is true that the Government did make some headway in negotiations with the Western powers, using the argument that only a strong and sovereign China could effectively resist the predatory designs of Japan. China was able to issue its first customs tariffs in 1930, although rates remained low. China gained some control over its Post Office and salt revenues, and in the foreign-endowed universities it was decreed that a Chinese must nominally exercise control. But the basic question of exterritoriality was not solved and foreign concessions and foreign troops remained on China's soil.

Chiang Kai-shek made no serious effort to introduce the much-needed reforms and he seemed unaware of the new economic, political and military disasters for which China was headed. Instead he wasted his finances, his energies and military reserves in 'extermination campaigns' against the Chinese Communists.

All these campaigns proved futile. Even under continuous attack the Chinese Communists increased their numbers, their influence and military strength. When Chiang Kai-shek first turned upon them in 1927 and broke their original organization, the movement was saved by opposition leaders within the party, including Mao Tse-tung, who advocated an alliance with the peasantry, confiscation of landlord property and the formation of a peasant-worker revolutionary army. The old party leaders were deposed in 1927 and Mao Tse-tung organized the Autumn Crop Uprising in Hunan, out of which came the 1st Division of the 1st Peasant and Workers' Army, drawing its recruits from the peasantry, the miners of Hangyang and insurrectionary troops of the Kuomintang.

Basing themselves on a vigorous land reform movement, the Communists defeated every attempt of Chiang Kai-shek to destroy them and their following. By 1934 they had established a large Soviet area in Kiangsi and beaten off five of Chiang Kai-shek's 'extermination campaigns'.

The War of Resistance

But towering over all other issues in China was still the menace of Japan. Chiang Kai-shek's feeble attempts to restore national sovereignty and his negotiations over the foreign concessions became academic when Japan threatened to make a concession of the whole of China. And the basic reforms which the Communists sought to introduce could hardly be realized without a country to practise them in.

Japan made clear that its intention was to dismember China piece by piece and place the whole country under Japanese tutelage in order to 'save the Chinese people from Communism'. That Chiang Kai-shek had already committed the bulk of his military forces against the Chinese Communists did not satisfy the Japanese. That the Western powers were not opposed to a limited Japanese expansion at the expense of China, primarily in the north-east, did not satisfy the Japanese either.

From the seizure of the three north-eastern provinces in 1931 and the creation of the fictitious state of 'Manchukuo', Japan proceeded with its design to conquer China as the first step in its grandiose master plan to dominate the world. A state of 'limited war' had begun.

Resistance in China accumulated slowly. In high places there were pro-Japanese officers, and there were some who relied upon support from the Western powers rather than on the native strength of their own country. Chiang Kai-shek was absorbed in his perpetual campaign to eliminate the Communist areas in Kiangsi, and in keeping a balance of power with the provincial war-lords.

Among the first to call for a war of resistance was the 'Young Marshal', Chang Hsueh-liang, who had been ordered by Nanking to withdraw his troops from the north-east when the Japanese entered in 1931. Then the 19th Route Army aroused the whole of China in 1932 when it repelled, on its own initiative, a Japanese naval assault on Shanghai. Following this, Madame Sun Yat-sen, the widow of the first President, helped found the National Salvation League which united many prominent Chinese patriots in a general call for resistance. In 1934 the Communist Red Army itself began to withdraw from Kiangsi, and executed its brilliant 6,000-mile Long March to the north-west, its Yenan base, choosing this strategic position to engage the Japanese.

This famous march was a strategic withdrawal and an advance. At its end there were only 20,000 survivors, but the Red Army had passed through provinces containing more than 200.000,000 people, spreading a militant propaganda, taxing the rich, distributing the goods of big landlords to the poor, and, at a time when the whole nation was becoming alive to the menace, proclaiming war against Japan.

In Shensi the Communists continued their agrarian revolution, and based their national policy on achieving unity among all patriotic Chinese who would join in a war of resistance.

Japan's steady encroachments from the north on China's territory continued unabated and unrestrained. While there were widespread demands that the Nanking Government accept the Communists' appeal for unity and national resistance, Chiang Kai-shek wavered. It was then, in December, 1936, that the famous Sian Incident occurred. Fearing that Chiang's indecision was playing into the hands of the Japanese, the Young Marshal arrested him and held him in Sian. After some anxious weeks Chiang was finally released, on the insistence of the Communists, the implicit terms being that he should lead the nation in resisting any further Japanese aggression.

War began in 1937. A truce was made between the Communists and

Chiang. In the long years of fighting both the Kuomintang and Communists made limited mutual concessions in striving for agreement. But it was not a happy marriage. The Communists did slow down their agrarian reform programme and ceased to confiscate landlord property, making an exception only of those landlords who co-operated with the Japanese. But their whole method of creating a peasant guerilla militia, starting co-operative factories, conducting popular agitation and talking of a new China after the war was an anathema to the Kuomintang.

On the other hand, Kuomintang troops were used for many years to blockade the Communists' Shensi-Kansu-Ninghsia Border Region instead of to fight the enemy, and there was a particularly acute crisis at the end of 1940 when extreme right-wing elements in the Kuomintang engineered an attack of the Communists' New Fourth Army, then operating against the Japanese south of the Yangtse.

The Kuomintang accused the Communists of using the war merely to extend their influence throughout China. The Communists replied that, in being the foremost and best fighters in the war of resistance, they naturally won the support of the Chinese people.

The truth is that the Chinese Communist Party and its renamed Joint Democratic Army did come out of the war greatly strengthened. Operating deep within the enemy's lines, especially in north China, the Communists drew millions of peasants into guerilla activity, liberated a major part of the countryside and brought social reform, education and a new sense of dignity to the peasant masses. The discipline and self-denial of the Communist soldier made him an outstanding propagandist for a new China.

On the other hand, the Kuomintang, centred upon Chungking, failed to produce an adequate social programme for the people. Socially it was on the defensive. The atmosphere of Chungking and Szechuan province was one of corruption and war-lordism. The Japanese seizure of the great coastal cities had undermined the strength of the Chinese industrialists who had been, in a sense, the one healthy influence within the Kuomintang. Chiang Kai-shek's adherents in Chungking were predominantly the landlord-gentry and provincial war-lords of the south-west; and, with them, a group of bureaucrats whose political influence enabled them to accumulate vast fortunes out of war-time contracts, speculation and jobbery. Chief among these were the groups headed by T. V. Soong, H. H, Kung and the 'CC Clique' of the notorious Chen brothers.

Civil War

One thing was certain: after VJ Day China's freedom could only be guaranteed by the establishment of a strong, democratic and popular central government, a government pledged to end civil war and to promote economic reconstruction.

The Kuomintang had its chance. In 1937 the Communist Party had declared: 'The Communist Party of China has not merely joined hands with the Kuomintang to save the nation during the war, but it is determined to cooperate harmoniously with the Kuomintang to reconstruct the nation after the war has ended in victory.' After VJ Day the Communists stood by this declaration.

When the war ended the Communists' Joint Democratic Army was in full control of some areas of the country, particularly in Shensi and the northeast (Manchuria). Here they set up provisional democratic governments. In north China, too, the Communists had liberated some areas from the Japanese. As far south as the West River and Hainan Island there were liberated areas controlled by Communist guerilla forces. Nevertheless, the Kuomintang controlled the bulk of China and had vastly superior military forces.

Chiang Kai-shek was faced with three alternatives. The first: to convene a popular Political Consultative Conference for the election of an all-party government, release political prisoners and reform the Kuomintang's clique-ridden administration. In this event, the Communist Party was prepared to turn over the areas under its control and its military forces to the new all-party government. The second: to come to local arrangements with the various liberated areas, sign truce agreements, and so recognize a sort of *status quo*. The third: to attempt the military subjugation of the liberated areas.

From the beginning it was apparent that Chiang would not accept the first alternative. But at times, particularly under the influence of American mediation, it seemed as though some attempt was to be made to reach truce agreements, to take the second path. In some parts of China agreements were actually reached. Yet those concerned were quick to realize that truce agreements were being used merely to regroup and build up forces for future attacks. In his White Paper, Dean Acheson explained America's role in the affair thus: The United States 'attempted to assist in working out a *modus vivendi* which would avert civil war but nevertheless preserve and even increase the influence of the Nationalist Government.' The so-called truce-makers were helping one side.

By June, 1946, the Kuomintang had launched full-scale civil war. The third and fatal alternative was chosen. The Kuomintang was riding the tiger.

What led it into this folly?

There were two factors, and the first has been explained by General Marshall: 'On the side of the Nationalist Government, which is in effect the Kuomintang Party, there is a dominant group of reactionaries who have been opposed, in my opinion, to almost every effort I have made to influence the formation of a genuine coalition government. This has usually been under the cover of political or party action, but since the party was the government, this action, though subtle and indirect, has been devastating in effect.' The reactionaries of the Kuomintang wished only to preserve their absolute power and enrich themselves through the exercise of this power. The welfare of China was not even a secondary consideration.

'Bureaucratic capitalism' has been no mere political slogan in post-war China. The Kuomintang was both incapable of organizing and unwilling to undertake the reconstruction of the national economy. Speculation replaced production. The Soong, Kung and Chen cliques made no effort to restore industrial production and they let the countryside go to rack and ruin. A large proportion of overseas aid went into the pockets of the bureaucrats. The Kuomintang 'recovery armies, seized grain and livestock on a large scale. Industrial production fell to pieces when Kuomintang civil and military officials took over. In the absence of any constructive plan and national control, the Kuomintang officials who had jurisdiction over industrial areas were free to strip and sell plant and raw materials.

The depredations of the Kuomintang did, in fact, such great damage to the whole national economy that the Chinese people were driven to the point where they could no longer tolerate the regime. Communists or no Communists, the people were ready to revolt. Chiang Kai-shek could only resort to further violence and repression.

The second factor that determined the launching of civil war was Chiang's belief that he would have the whole strength of the United States behind him in any action he might take against the Communists. As Dean Acheson wrote of the Kuomintang and its Government: 'In the opinion of many observers they had sunk into corruption, into a scramble for place and power, and into reliance on the United States to win the war for them and to preserve their own domestic supremacy.'

American relations with the Kuomintang Government were very close indeed. It is enough evidence to note that official figures issued from Washington at the beginning of 1948 put aid given to Chiang after VJ Day at $1,400,000,000. Warships, other vessels and ammunition amounted to $800,000,000 in addition (according to a Washington *Associated Press* dispatch, February 25, 1948). Undisclosed aid is assumed to be much higher. After VJ Day the American Army undertook what was then the biggest airlift in history, transporting Kuomintang armies to various civil-war fronts. President Truman said officially that the transport of four Kuomintang armies alone to the northeast front cost the United States $300,000,000.

Why did America spend such colossal sums to ensure overwhelming Kuomintang military strength, particularly in the north-east?

Examining the matter coldly, it seems that the following extract from a report issued by the influential Foreign Policy Association in New York on November 15, 1947, gives the answer: 'In Washington China is viewed primarily as the strategic factor in the relations between the United States of America and the Soviet Union ... In a military sense, China, along with southern Korea, thus becomes an adjunct of Japan. Since Nanking has proved that it is unable to bring an entire country under its rule, policymakers are encouraged to think of China not as a unit but as a composite of bases and zones of varying military significance...'

It is not to be imagined that the Kuomintang was simply the willing tool of an American imperialism, and that Kuomintang armies executed all their moves at Washington's command. The Kuomintang cliques were playing their own game of loot and aggrandizement. Nor is it to be imagined that the United States Government and its military staffs had well-defined strategic plans. Further, America had an economic as well as a military interest in China. The various trade and commercial agreements from 1946 through 1948 were of some importance to the United States Government. The Sino-American Bilateral Agreement signed on July 3, 1948, stipulated among other things that: 'The Government of China will facilitate the transfer to the United States for stockpiling and other purposes materials originating in China which are required by the United States of America as a result of deficiencies or potential deficiencies in its own resources...'

However, with these economic considerations and confusion of strategic thinking, there was the underlying attitude of the 'policymakers' that China was not a nation, a people who desired life, liberty and happiness, but a series of military bases for 'containing Communism', with the north-east the key base of them all. Various groups exerted pressure on Chiang. He himself made the decision to attack, misled by his advisers and deceived by his own incredible megalomania.

In July, as fighting spread, the North-east Bureau of the Communist Party and the Joint Democratic Army began a broad movement for land reform. A great deal of land nominally belonged to the Japanese and big puppets. This land was made subject to immediate confiscation. Because of the whole nature of the absentee landholding system in the north-east, and land confiscation during the Japanese occupation, land reform was popularly supported and went ahead rapidly. At first the best officers and men of the Joint Democratic Army took part in the work. It is said that their commander-in-chief,

General Lin Piao, considered the land reform movement more important than winning or losing a few battles. Indeed, as fighting progressed, the Joint Democratic Army drew immense strength from the popular support it won through land reform. Victory was to be with those whose policy answered the needs of the Chinese peasantry and the whole Chinese people.

By February, 1948, Chiang had completely lost the initiative in the northeast. He had, in fact, lost the initiative as far south as the approaches to the Yangtse. By October, 1948, the Joint Democratic Army (now called the Chinese People's Liberation Army) had put out of action 540,000 Kuomintang troops. No amount of American aid could stem the tide. The Chinese people *were* moving with the impact of revolution. Chiang had defaulted as leader of the Chinese nation. He had forfeited the mantle of Sun Yat-sen, and it had passed to the Communists and their chairman, Mao Tse-tung.

Chapter Four

CHINA'S COMMUNISTS

How should one describe the Chinese Communists? Can it be said that they 'are fed with the same food, hurt with the same weapons, subject to the same diseases, healed by the same means, warmed by the same winter and summer, as a Christian is?' Or are they kindly fanatics, some pro-Russian and some pro-West, a new Mandarinate or possessors of split personalities as various commentators have suggested?

In the wake of the Liberation Army a new type of man came to Shanghai. They were the *kangpu*, the cadres. Not all of the new 'officialdom' of Shanghai were Communist Party members, but the Communists were the leading elements and they established customs, methods and habits for all directors and employees of Government and public organisations.

To Shanghai's worldly-wise citizens the newly arrived officials seem a strange lot indeed. The sober men and bobbed-haired women in dusty blue uniforms who sat behind the desks in the municipal offices or worked in the manager's office of the city's banks were too naïve to be true. How, people asked each other, could one deal with officials who showed no interest in 'squeeze' or commissions? Was a Government servant worth his salt if he didn't make the best financial use of his position, and wasn't it unfilial or unfriendly if he didn't take advantage of his authority to get his relatives and

31

acquaintances easy and secure jobs in the Government? And, after all, what could these fellows really know about running a city when they had spent many years of their lives in one-horse villages with uneducated peasants? And what were round-faced girls doing in important posts?

Yet Shanghai was forced to concede that here was a new group, new individuals whose standards were not comparable with any privileged Mandarinate officialdom of the old China. Just as the men of the Communists' armies have proved themselves the very reverse of the traditional Chinese soldier, so the blue-jacketed officials have begun to stand out as the example of a radically different type of ruler.

Some of them have come from wealthy homes, even from the best schools and universities of Shanghai itself, but all have adopted a new and spartan routine of communal working and living. All of them eat in one of three standard 'kitchens': 'Big Kitchen' for the majority of the personnel, giving each of them enough daily rice, enough cooking oil, and a few pence for vegetables (enough perhaps to buy half a cabbage), with a pound or so of meat a month to each person; 'Middle' and 'Little Kitchen' for certain special categories such as the higher officials and those doing extra-heavy work, only slightly more luxurious. General Chen Yi, mayor of Shanghai and commander of the Third Field Army, will have no more than two small bowls of vegetables, or meat and a soup, with his midday rice. The Communists do not stop at simple food rations. All wear the one type of uniform, and each receives one summer suit of light cotton, one winter suit of padded clothes.

In living a communal life the Communists have a certain security in that their health, their children's schooling and their housing—of the sparest— are taken care of. They also receive a monthly issue of cigarettes, toothpaste, soap and a face towel. But no one has more than the monthly allowance of something under 10s. to put in his or her purse, sufficient to buy a few extra cigarettes, or a book or two, or a pair of shoes. When it comes to household duties, they do the work themselves; although in cases where a mother is working and may not be able to attend to very young children, an *amah* (servant-nurse) may be provided where there is no nursery.

The rigorous communal life carries over into their work. From six o'clock in the morning, when two hours of study and discussion take them to breakfast, to the late hours of the night, when matters of administration pre-occupy them, there is no let-up. No wonder some of the ex-Kuomintang officials, who have been kept on in government work, are heard to murmur: '*T'ai lihai*—too formidable, too formidable!'

The individual Communist believes that he should sacrifice personal benefits for the sake of his cause, that he should be 'the first to bear the sorrows of the revolution but the last to enjoy its fruits'. But the Communists do not regard themselves as saints or martyrs. Their way of life and their sacrifices are not intended to set them above the common people of China. They have no intention of becoming a new Madarinate, a self-perpetuating body of officials. Their frugal living is not designed to set them apart from the ordinary folk of China: on the contrary, it is meant to place them on the same level as the mass of the peasantry and the workers, to identify them with the great body of the Chinese people whom they serve. Today there are five million party members and most of them have been recruited since 1945. Naturally there are as wide a variety of types, personalities and individuals among these new recruits as are to be found in all China; but nevertheless the standards set by the old-timers do become the rule for every new member. The young Communists rapidly identify themselves with the collective living and action of their party. Since the end of 1949 admission has become increasingly difficult to obtain, and no doubt many 'careerists' and 'opportunists' who decided to join because victory seemed assured will soon find themselves outside the ranks.

The Communists are a firmly united force with a strict regimen, but this does not mean that they are depressingly uncritical or lack initiative. An acquaintance of mine, who had worked in an inland medical mission, once said that the older Yenan Communists were much more likeable than the young upstarts who carried slogans about in their pockets and had no concern for people's feelings. On the other hand, I have heard an older Communist lament that she could not keep up with the youth, that she was burdened with

NORTH-WEST CHINA

1 Sinkiang	4 Ninghsia
2 Chinghai	5 Suiyuan
3 Kansu	6 Shensi

NORTH CHINA

7 Shansi	9 Hopei
8 Charhar	10 Pingyuan

NORTH-EAST CHINA

11 Inner Mongolian
    Autonomous Area

12 Jehol	15 Kirin
13 Heilungkiang	16 Liaotung
14 Liaohsi	17 Sungkiang

SOUTH-WEST CHINA

18 Sikang	20 Szechuan
19 Yunnan	21 Kweichow

CENTRAL-SOUTH CHINA

22 Honan	25 Kiangsi
23 Hupei	26 Kwangsi
24 Hunan	

27 Kwangtung (with
    Hainan Island)

EAST CHINA

28 Shantung	30 Anhwei
29 Kiangsu	31 Chekiang

32 Fukien (with Taiwan)

backward habits and old-fashioned ideas that hampered her in the expanding universe of the new China.

China is not standing still, solidifying into a new rigid order. Neither have the Chinese Communists reached the end of their evolution. And the point is that they realize it. To overcome the rather natural inertia of the older members, to allow for the development of new people and to deal with ever-changing national problems, there is a great deal of inner party discussion, criticism and self-criticism. This goes on continually and covers everything from the smallest details of personal behaviour to the largest questions of national policy, which the rank and file may have little say in formulating but which are invariably discussed at length until they are unanimously accepted.

To Serve the People

With all this discussion and debate, criticism and revision, what do the Communists hold to as the constant criterion in action? There is no better interpreter of Communism in China than Mao Tse-tung, and he writes on this point in his thesis on *Coalition Government*: 'Our starting-point is to serve the Chinese people earnestly and wholeheartedly, and never to be severed from the people; to set out always from the point of view of serving people's interests, not serving the interests of a small group or oneself; and to give equal responsibility to the people and the guiding organization...'

In the last phrase is the key to the method of the Chinese Communists. The 'guiding organization' is the Communist Party; and yet the Communists think of themselves as no more than guides to the masses of the people, who are carrying out the revolution for themselves. There is a revealing passage in an article *On the Party* written in 1945 by Liu Shao-chi, who is perhaps second in standing to Mao Tse-tung in the Chinese Communist Party, and also a Vice-Chairman of the present Government. Liu Shao-chi writes: 'The masses of the people make their own history. Their emancipation must be based on their own consciousness and willingness. They select their own vanguard. And, under the leadership of this vanguard, they must organize themselves and fight for their emancipation by their own efforts'.

To Western ears, to those who are accustomed to a very different democratic process, all this may sound a mere juggling with words, a game of dialectics. But it has a very real meaning in China, where the Communists began to have their first real successes when they won the leadership of spontaneous peasant uprisings, identified themselves with the cause of the peasantry and created the conditions for social change in China through the agrarian revolution. It has a very real meaning now when the Communists are relying for the consolidation and further advance of their revolution upon the full support, enthusiasm and labour of the industrial workers of the great cities. These are the people for whom the revolution is to be made, and 'the people' is no figure of speech but the living peasants and workers of China with all their individual hopes and needs. And it is interesting to note that Liu Shao-chi uses the dictum: 'An ordinary person is *ipso facto* often nearer to the truth than some of our higher bodies.'

Are they really true Communists? Are they Marxists? Are they not merely Chinese reformers? The standard answer, as it is given in China, is: 'The policies of the Chinese Communist Party were all formulated under the brilliant leadership of the party's great leader, Comrade Mao Tse-tung, who has successfully integrated the ideas and ideals of Marx, Engels, Lenin and Stalin with the concrete conditions of the Chinese revolution. It is under the banner of Mao Tse-tung that the party and the people have passed from victory to victory.'

If we want a more specific answer then we may proceed to consider what is the 'banner of Mao Tse-tung' and what is the nature of the man himself.

Heaven Will Not Delay a Traveller

Few Chinese come closer to Mao Tse-tung than a place in the mass celebrations in Peking or a seat in a Shanghai cinema. But when the deliberate rotund figure with a boyish smile and blurred Hunanese accent does appear on the cinema screens, then there is a volley of applause. He has the poise of a scholar, the slow mannerisms of a peasant, and he fires the imagination of his audience like a poet.

Mao Tse-tung is fifty-seven this year. He was born in a peasant village in the province of Hunan in 1893. Until last year he had never travelled outside China, although he knows his own country intimately. His progress has been rather that of a continual absorption of every stimulus and idea—from Chinese history, from Western science, from Sun Yat-sen, front Marxism, from the lives of peasants, teachers and workers—that might serve to remake China; and, as one of his favourite sayings has it, Heaven will not delay a traveller.

Man's father was a poor peasant who, by engaging in trading and other enterprises, managed in his lifetime to become relatively 'rich'. Young Mao was the scholar of the family, who was sent to school but who worked in the fields in the early morning and at night. At school and at home Mao was taught and drilled in the Confucian classics, but he and his school-friends preferred to read the popular romances of Chinese history, the stories of warriors and rebellions. Yet these tales disturbed Mao because in them he found no peasant heroes. At that time he came across a book called *Shen Shih Wei-yen* (Words of Warning), which placed the blame for China's misfortunes on her lack of Western science and technology. This set Mao thinking and, after a quarrel with his rather despotic father, he left home and became a restless seeker after knowledge.

Books were not the sole stimulus in his early life. As a poor student in the period of the 1911 revolution he saw hungry rebellious peasants executed and Changsha taken by a rebel army. He himself became a soldier. When the 1911 revolution ended with the withdrawal of Sun Yat-sen, Mao again became a traveller and a student.

There is a dramatic quality in Mao Tse-tung's life and it can read like the whole history of the Chinese national revolution. All the influences that inspired the young patriotic Chinese were critically accepted by Mao, with the difference that he reacted to them most vigorously and could not wait to put them into practice. In 1917 he helped to found the *Hsin Min Hsueh Hui* (New People's Study Society), some of whose members were to become famous names in Chinese Communism. In 1918 he was in Peking, assistant librarian at the National University, interested in anarchism and helping to send revolutionary students abroad to France and Germany. In 1919 he was prominent in student organizations, an advocate of social reformation, the Munroe Doctrine and independence for his native province of Hunan. By 1920 he had come under the influence of the early Chinese Marxists and read the first Marxist book to be translated into Chinese, the *Communist Manifesto*.

From that time forward Mao regarded himself as a Marxist and his life becomes identified with the growth of the Kungchantang, the Chinese Communist Party, whose first meeting he attended in Shanghai in May, 1921.

From being one of a group of early Communist leaders, Mao Tse-tung emerged as the most provident thinker of Chinese Communism and its best organizer. It was Mao Tse-tung who saw most dearly that the Chinese peasantry, far from being an 'inert mass', were quantitatively the greatest revolutionary force in China. He led the first organized peasant uprisings and set off the great land reform movement. He led the Chinese Communists to Yenan and worked out their immensely popular 'united front' policy against Japan. It was Mao Tse-tung who realized that China's national revolution could succeed only as an armed struggle, accumulating forces strong enough to meet all internal and external resistance, strong enough to defeat reaction at home and imperialism abroad. He and Chu Teh organized the Chinese Red Army and the People's Liberation Army.

Above all, Mao was the architect of the policies of New Democracy that have united the Chinese people in the new China of which Sun Yat-sen dreamed, a China sovereign, united, democratic and strong.

It is almost as though the culture and abilities of a great people were reflected in the many-sided personality of one man. Yet, in spite of current theories to the contrary, Mao Tse-tung is not a new Emperor; nor is his party a new and sinewy version of the old, imperial dynasties. The Chinese Communists *are* revolutionaries and theirs *is* a new China. They exist not to fill an old throne decorated with modern trimmings but to abolish thrones altogether. On the 28th anniversary of the establishment of the Chinese Communist Party Mao Tse-tung said this: 'As a man passes from childhood to youth, from youth to manhood, and then at last from manhood to old age, so the Chinese

Communist Party has its ages. Today the Chinese Communist Party is no longer a child, nor a young stripling in its teens, but is come to manhood. In the course of time a man becomes old, then dies. And this is true for a political party. When classes are abolished there will be no further need for instruments that serve in the class struggle and for the forms of State that serve in class and national struggle. We are unlike the political parties of the bourgeoisie which fear to speak of the abolition of classes and the end of party power. We openly declare that this is the end for which we are struggling.'

Mao Tse-tung measures each act and theory of today against the scale of a far-ranging future. Each effort of the Communists is a small addition to the large and all-embracing design of a 'harmonious universe'. Mao believes that the Chinese should look far into the future and comprehend the whole situation of the world. Their vision should have both depth and breadth. As for each action that is taken today, Mao Tse-tung writes: 'Without a comprehensive view of the situation as a whole there is no possibility of making a single decisive move on the chessboard ... and the whole world situation is the ultimate guide.'

Before we consider the moves that Mao Tse-tung, the political philosopher and military strategist, is making on the chessboard today and his Marxism as it is applied in China, it would be a loss if we neglected another of his accomplishments. According to some, Mao Tse-tung is one of the foremost poets of modern China, though Mao himself disclaims the title and regards his 'wind-sand' poems as an idle game. He writes in the classical style, and among his few poems that have been published this is perhaps the most revealing. It was written during an aeroplane journey across north China in 1945:

Spring-drenched Garden
North-country scene—
Leagues icy waste
More leagues snowbound
(See the Great Wall winding)

Quite desolate,
Wide river Ho
Its torrents stilled
Hill's frozen snake
Wax elephants,
(Lo, we are Heaven climbing)
Until spring days
Shall earth unveil
In all her beauty.
Hill river loveliness
Won countless heroes' reverence.

Pity Ch'in and Han's*
Unlearned state.
T'ang and Sung Kings
Lacked all feeling.
Imperial
Genghis Khan
Could but bend bow at eagles.
All is past—
Only today
The truly great.

---

* *Early emperors of China.*

Chapter Five

NEW DEMOCRACY TAKES SHAPE

O_N THE morning after the fighting ended in Shanghai we turned on the radio wondering what changes there would be. How would the new order announce itself? Tuning in we heard—a Methodist morning service, a band playing 'Men of Harlech', Soviet marches, Buddhist chanting, American dance music, and some new *yangko** songs.

Then there was an announcement to the people of Shanghai:

1. All citizens and their property will be protected, but public order must be observed.
2. Private industrial and commercial property will be protected.
3. Public utilities, schools and churches, including all personnel therein, will be protected.
4. Property of the bogus Kuomintang Government and of the Four Big Families—Chiang, Soong, Kung and Chen—will be confiscated.
5. Foreigners, with the exception of those violating the law and sheltering criminal elements, will be protected.
6. The hoarding of arms and ammunition is prohibited.
7. Troops of the People's Liberation Army are not permitted to obtain

---

* *A traditional peasant dance which has become very popular in the new China.*

anything from the people without payment.

All citizens were then requested to go back to work, to start the factories and to help the new Military Control Commission to promote 'business as usual'.

Shanghai was somewhat dazed by the speed of it all, but the start was reassuring. In the streets the shutters came down. Children clambered over the wrecked armoured-cars and half-tracks. The sandbag emplacements at the street corners were spilling open in the fine rain. On the Bund, opposite the massive frontage of the Hong Kong-Shanghai Bank, students lectured and distributed leaflets to a milling crowd of dock-workers and passers-by. Trucks decorated with banners and greenery carried other student groups from point to point in the city, lecturing and singing. With them went dance teams, girls in gay costumes with drums and cymbals, who danced the peasant *yangko* and acted short propaganda plays. There was an easy holiday mood.

But behind the scenes all was not so carefree. Shanghai's economy was prostrate. Few factories could operate. Most of the gold, silver and foreign currency reserves of the banks had been looted by fleeing Kuomintang officials. The currency in circulation was valueless. Most of the port's shipping had been taken to Formosa or scuttled in the Whangpoo river. And the city was down to rockbottom in its essential supplies. The Kuomintang administration had been frankly dependent on outside help, E C A supplying some 50 per cent of the city's rice requirements and thousands of bales of raw cotton and cotton yarn to keep Shanghai's textile industries going. Now, not only was E C A aid withdrawn, but large shipments of E C A supplies had been previously diverted in anticipation of the changeover. To add to official headaches, Shanghai's population of six millions, together with the new multitudes of refugees, was double the number that the city could productively employ.

First Things First

The fundamental test of the ability of the new authorities to govern lay in the stabilization of currency, as chronic inflation had been the rule under the previous Government. As early as the end of May the Communists' *Jen Min Piao* was issued for circulation as the legal tender, and conversion of the Kuomintang so-called *Gold Yuan* notes was started at the rate of GY, 100,000 to J M P, 1. The conversion was carried out smoothly, and after June 6 there was no sign of any Gold Yuan in the city.

However, during the first weeks of the changeover, before a foreign exchange rate had been set and before commodities began to flow in from the countryside, the J M P began to inflate rapidly. Fuel was added to the flames by an undetermined number of 'disruptive elements' left behind by the Kuomintang with instructions to sabotage the economy of the new regime. Undoubtedly some of the spectacular price rises of the first few weeks were due to the alarming rumours circulated by some of these elements, who mixed with the silver dollar pedlars, thousands of whom thronged Shanghai's pavements, and whose very existence was a continual threat to currency stabilization. Early rumours of aerial bombing, of blockade by the Kuomintang navy, and the outbreak of a third world war caused some panic. People hastened to sell their J M P for silver. The local Chinese press began to print strong editorials urging the authorities to take action against this black market. The situation was critical.

Thereupon Shanghai had its first demonstration of the Communists' policy that public reforms must be 'consciously and voluntarily taken up by the people themselves'. Instead of sending out a gendarmerie to round up the silver dollar pedlars and shoot several as an example—in the manner of the Kuomintang—the Communists launched a political campaign designed to impress upon the public the detrimental effects of the silver black market.

Students paraded through the streets carrying banners criticizing the pedlars and those citizens who patronized them. Meetings were held in offices and factories. Soap-box orators harangued the city pedestrian, giving him elementary lectures in economics and pointing out the harmful effects of silver dollar speculation upon the city's economy. Plays and skits were performed in the streets. The radio, the daily press and the cinemas took up the campaign. Political workers spoke to the pedlars themselves, attempting to make them see the light. Finally the police arrested a few of the more obdurate. But even this display of force was different from the old days. In cases where the arrested pedlars could prove themselves 'legitimate' traders, they were warned and their capital of silver coins was returned to them. Shanghai was actually persuaded to forego the silver black market. The Communists' belief in public education and public cooperation in action succeeded.

Simultaneously the authorities dealt with the problem of foreign exchange. The reorganized Bank of China dropped the old fixed rate of exchange and began to quote a daily rate, with the approval of the East China Office of the People's Bank. This measure was adopted to avoid the possibility of continual gaps between the official rate and a black market rate, always a crucial problem in Kuomintang times. Because the new rate was kept at a realistic daily level, it succeeded in wiping out the currency black market.

The measure taken to protect savings bank deposits was another wise move. Depositors received credit for a certain number of Parity Units on the money, gold, silver and notes, that they handed in. These Parity Units (still in operation) are calculated on the daily market price of the four basic commodities—medium-grade rice, coal, cooking oils, and cotton cloth. When one wishes to withdraw his or her original deposit, it is paid out according to the number of Units originally deposited. Thus, if the prices of commodities rise (i.e. money depreciates), the depositor loses nothing, since he is paid according to the market prices prevailing on the day of withdrawal. In addition, the bank pays interest. This Parity Unit system still operates, and all wages are paid in Units, thus guaranteeing the real value of income.

In spite of considerable shortages and a prevailing state of war, these and similar financial measures have been successfully carried out. Public confidence in the J M P currency has been secured generally throughout China. For China, where inflation and other chronic monetary disorders have frequently crippled economic progress, the importance of this achievement cannot be underestimated. People's Livelihood, the third but perhaps the most important of Sun Yat-sen's Three People's Principles, was forthrightly applied from the beginning.

Of course, the currency problem could not have been solved permanently by the measures described above. Centralization of the national finances, the success of land reform, the restoration of trade and industry, and especially the efficient central control and distribution of grain have all been necessary to effect a permanent solution. But I have stressed this initial currency stabilization because of its individual importance and because it was the first palpable example of Mao Tse-tung's policy of 'New Democracy' in action.

The Principle of Democracy

'New Democracy' implies more than economic reforms; it implies a new political system. Within three weeks of the changeover in Shanghai the first steps were taken towards the formation of a new central government for China. In Peking on June 15, on the initiative of the Communist Party, a preparatory committee was formed to prepare a Political Consultative Conference for the whole of China and to draw up plans for the formation of a central government. This government, according to Mao Tse-tung, was to be a 'democratic coalition government'.

In Peking, Mao Tse-tung was made chairman of the steering committee elected to organize the Political Consultative Conference, and his deputy chairmen were: Chou En-lai (Communist Party), Marshal Li Chi-sen (chairman of the Revolutionary Committee of the Kuomintang), Shen Chun-ju (responsible leader of the Democratic League of China and noted jurist), Kuo Mo-jo (non-party writer), and Chen Hsu-teng (publisher and director of Shanghai's Commercial Press).

The convocation of a Political Consultative Conference was first proposed by the Chinese Communist Party one year before, in May, 1948. It was not a makeshift arranged to exploit the favourable military situation and the rapid disintegration of Kuomintang authority. It was part of a stated policy. In fact, the proposal to form a 'democratic coalition government' had done much to cut the ground from under the Kuomintang in the latter stages of the civil war. China desperately needed national unity and economic recovery could not be delayed. Chiang Kai-shek and the Kuomintang cliques had proved themselves time and again to be intractable, unrepentent sinners against the body of China. The United States policy of aid to the Kuomintang had again roused fear and hatred of foreign 'imperialist intervention' in China's affairs. On the grounds of patriotism alone, a great many responsible citizens were ready to consult with the Communist Party. Who else had a policy, the strength and the will to unite China? Months before the liberation of Shanghai, representatives of the Democratic League, the Revolutionary Committee of the Kuomintang, and other parties had been in conference with the Communists in Peking. To Peking had gone such influential Chinese as Madame Sun Yat-sen, Chang Chih-chung (former Kuomintang governor of Sinkiang), and Tan Kah-kee (chairman of the Association of Overseas Chinese in the South Seas, resident of Singapore). General Fu Tso-yi, the most able of the Kuomintang's strategists and commander of all the Kuomintang forces in north China, went over to the Communist side in December, 1948, with all his armies.

The Communists were masters of the situation. And yet they had no intention of setting up a one-party dictatorship. They could not do so. They *were* masters of the situation *because* their policies and their leadership were acceptable to many different factions and democratic parties.

In his 1940 essay on *New Democracy*, Mao Tse-tung had enunciated the doctrine that China should have a transitional government of 'all the revolutionary classes'. He considered that China's historical situation made this necessary, and when their opportunity came in 1949 the Communists proceeded to translate this doctrine into action. Politically they intended to share power: and the Political Consultative Conference was the chosen method.

It is illuminating therefore to study the detailed membership of the Chinese People's Political Consultative Conference (its make-up was decided by Mao Tse-tung's steering committee), which held its first plenary session in Peking on September 23, 1949:

The composition of the P P C C, which was to elect the new Central People's Government of China, is a guide to the salient features of political 'New Democracy'.

Non-Communist Parties

All parties which have at one time or another opposed the Kuomintang's one-party government were represented in the P P C C. Some of the parties are very loosely organized and their membership uncounted, but they each stand for a sector of Chinese political opinion within China or abroad.

The two most important non-Communist parties are the Revolutionary Committee of the Kuomintang and the Democratic League of China. Since the first meeting of the P P C C, several of the smaller groupings have united with one or other of these two major parties. The National Salvation

Association, for example, dissolved its organization and the majority of its members have joined the Democratic League.

The origins of the Revolutionary Committee of the Kuomintang go back to the time in 1924 when Sun Yat-sen led a coalition government, including Communists, and announced popular and broad policies against feudalism and foreign intervention in China. Sun Yat-sen was, after all, the founder of the Kuomintang. The more honest and patriotic of Sun's associates in the Kuomintang did not forget his principles. Li Chi-sen and Madame Sun Yat-sen were among these. Li Chi-sen was one of the leaders of the heroic 19th Route Army which defended Shanghai against the Japanese attack in 1932. He continued to oppose Chiang Kai-shek's conciliatory attitude to Japan. In 1934 he and his associates actually revolted against Chiang and established in Fukien a 'Federal Revolutionary Government of China' that was in many ways like the present Central People's Government. It was short-lived, but from that time Li Chi-sen was led by his intense patriotism from attempts to reform the Kuomintang to the formation of the Revolutionary Committee of the Kuomintang in 1948, dedicated to fight Chiang Kai-shek's 'treacherous and dictatorial regime'.

Li Chi-sen is now one of the six Vice-Chairmen of the Central People's Government. His party may be said to speak for the interests of the 'patriotic bourgeoisie' in China, industrialists, former members of the Kuomintang, even some of the older provincial leaders who have made their stand on the issue of nationalism.

The Democratic League of China took shape in 1941 when, as one of its spokesmen said, it seemed that 'a new split between the Kuomintang and the Communist Party, as well as the probability of the former's return to the old course of appeasing Japan and waging war on Chinese, would eventually end in the capitulation of China'. Like Li Chi-sen's followers, the League was opposed to all foreign imperialism. The League played an honourable part in keeping China in the war at a time of crisis, and its advocacy of unconditional resistance to Japan was coupled with a demand for the liberalization of China's government, military forces and educational system. It was the party of China's intelligentsia, the inheritor of the old traditions of the scholar in Chinese civil life, lost in the corruption and violence of the nineteenth and early twentieth centuries.

The League suffered bitter persecution under the Kuomintang, during and after the anti-Japanese war. The much-admired Professor Wen I-to, assassinated by Kuomintang soldiers in 1946, was one of its more prominent supporters. The Kuomintang Government ordered the League's suppression in 1947, and, from then on, it was committed to co-operation with the Communist Party and to the overthrow of the Kuomintang as the only road to the liberal reforms for which it stood.

Today the Democratic League has several hundred thousand members. It has its own press in China and abroad. Its elder statesman, Chang Lan (rescued by underground workers from threat of assassination in Shanghai on the eve of that city's liberation) is a Vice-Chairman of the Central People's Government. Shen Chun-ju, who represented the League on Mao Tse-tung's steering committee, is now Chief Justice of the Chinese Supreme Court.

Government of the People

Early this year I visited a once famous and busy café on Shanghai's Chung Cheng Road (now Yenan Road). In the course of conversation, the proprietress, a Mrs. Y—, said to myself and friend: 'Why are the Communists so strong? Who supports them?' And sadly she recalled the palmy days when every language on earth could be heard at her bar.

It is doubtful whether Mrs. Y—was well informed about the P P C C, but if she had studied the list of delegates' organizations would she really have been impressed to read that the All-China Federation of Natural Scientists or even the Shanghai Association of Civic Bodies was represented in the highest councils of the land? What on earth were these organizations? Where did they come from? Ordinary citizens had never taken part in politics in China.

But that is all past now. Millions of China's citizens live and breathe politics, all the more eagerly because it is for the first time. 'Liberation' is intensely political. Trade may have fallen off at the cafés on Chung Cheng

Road; but the halls and theatres of Shanghai are crammed day and night with citizens arguing and voting at meetings of the textile workers' unions, co-operative women's guilds, the student-teachers' federation, the Ancient Objets d'Art Custodian Committee, and committees *ad infinitum.*

It is true that the Communists have been responsible for initiating much of this activity, and here perhaps is the answer to Mrs. Y—'s heartfelt query. The Chinese Communists are strong not because they have curtailed democracy in China, but because they have extended it. Whoever helps form a trade union (or any public organization) is more likely to win the support of its membership than persons who have neglected public democracy,

On this subject the following has been written: 'The number of party delegates (at the 1949 People's Political Consultative Conference) constitutes only 28 per cent of the total delegation, while the number of delegates from the various mass organizations and civic bodies makes up approximately 40 per cent of the total. This big representation of the various mass organizations is indicative of the broad basis the conference will have among the people, and it will also strengthen the position of the Chinese Communist Party at the conference because most of these mass organizations are under the leadership of Communists or democratic leaders, and their members have long been sympathetic with the Communist programme.'*

As with beauty, democracy is often in the eye of the beholder. All will agree that it is a relative quality. But when we consider democracy in China we should avoid two common preconceptions. Democracy in China is not regarded as equivalent to the existence of various political parties. I have pointed out that there are several important non-Communist parties in the new China. These are by no means a facade. But I would emphasize again the political importance given to public organizations, trade unions, farmers', professional and businessmen's associations. They have at least as high a political status as actual political parties in effecting government by the people under New Democracy.

---

* Monthly Report. (*Millard Publishing Company, Shanghai, June,1949.*)

The second preconception is that predominance of the Communist Party is equivalent to one-party dictatorship or to the lessening of democratic liberties. Actually the Communists are eager that all other parties and groups should take an active part in running the country, if for no other reason than they realize that the success of their whole policy relies on the willing co-operation of the whole people. As a result, never before in China has there been such a popular stirring, such freedom of speech, such a quantity of public participation in the running of civic, regional and national affairs.

Democracy both practical and formal has begun. The calling of the P P C C was but the first step. It was not regarded as a finished or ideal democratic form. It was an attempt to achieve the widest possible representation of public feeling at the time.

Chapter Six

CHINA STANDS UP

SEPTEMBER, 1949, was a memorable month in China's history. In Peking a new Republic was founded, a new government elected, radically new laws and statutes adopted. The P P C C did all this and found time to choose a new flag, to declare Peking the capital of the new China and to adopt the Gregorian calendar.

In his opening address to the conference, Mao Tse-tung said: 'We have a feeling in common that our work will be written down in the history of mankind. It will say: the Chinese people, one quarter of humanity, from this time forth stood up!'

The conference met in the red-pillared halls of the Imperial Palace, in the very heart of China's ancient history. It had a touch of splendour about it, yet there were slogans on the walls which read: 'Practicability is the essence.'

There were present a 21-year-old student and 92-year-old Admiral Sa Chen-ping; four generations within one room. There were over sixty women delegates. There were old peasant women, and there were Kuomintang generals; there were tribesmen from the far south-west, and mechanics from the industrial north-east; there were Christians, Marxists, Buddhists and Mohammedans; there were famous novelists, and businessmen from Shanghai.

54

I met several of the Shanghai delegates shortly after their return from Peking. They all agreed that the meaning of the conference and the essence of the new China was summed up in Mao Tse-tung's words: 'China has stood up!' It meant that China would no longer be an 'insulted nation'; that one hundred years of corruption and agony, of foreign aggression and weak despotic governments, had come to all end.

We Chinese, said one of the delegates, 'have been likened in the past to a tray of loose sand, loose shifting sand. Now we have become a rock.'

He continued: 'One had to be in the meeting-hall watching the 600-odd delegates to understand what the united front means. There weren't only the eminent and educated people one might expect to see. There were old country women who could neither read nor write but who could tell the whole assembly precisely what the revolution meant to them. But everyone had made some contribution to the democratic movement in China. Even Fu Tso-yi was there. He made his contribution when he turned Peking over peacefully to the People's Liberation Army and encouraged other Kuomintang generals to do the same with their armies... Everyone worked hard at the conference and very seriously. The main task was to agree on a social, political and economic programme for the new China. We had to embody the united front of all democratic parties and groups into a Common Programme for the new China, and the programme that we did finally agree on contains all the policies that China will follow in the next three years.'

Another delegate explained: 'Some people wanted to include welfare provisions in the Common Programme, but it was felt that we would not be able to institute any widespread welfare activities in the initial period. Neither could we promise to wipe out illiteracy. We could only state that mass education would be promoted. The Common Programme is a cashable cheque: every word in it can be fulfilled.

'In the same way the programme suits the speed of all members of the united front. At first some delegates were impatient and wanted to mention China's going forward to socialism. Then it was pointed out that we are not yet ready for socialism and that to include it among our immediate goals

would only confuse matters. Another suggestion was that we accept dialectical materialism as a doctrine. This, too, was rejected on the grounds that
many people, such as Christians, could not agree with it. Everything in the
Common Programme was fully discussed and carefully worked out, and thus
when delegates voted they knew why they voted and why each policy was a
good thing.'

The methods used in shaping the Common Programme were those of
consultation rather than those of formal parliamentary procedure. First, the
draft programme drawn up by the P P C C's preparatory committee was distributed to delegates, and Chou En-lai gave a four-hour report on its provisions.
Then delegates met in their own small groups—for example, the journalists
met as one group, the Democratic League representatives met as another.
Discussion in these small groups was unrestricted and informal. It brought
forth many suggestions that were to be incorporated in the finished programme.
One woman delegate from Shanghai, who had had some experience of the
Chinese Industrial Co-operative Movement, objected to a weakness in the
draft programme's statement on co-operatives. She maintained that producers' co-operatives should be included as worthy of State support. Although
she voiced a minority opinion within her own group, her suggestions were
duly recorded and may be seen in the final draft of the programme.

The conference steering committee correlated the ideas brought forward
in the small groups, revised the draft and then reported to the full conference.
The assembly then broke up again, this time into mixed groups of some 40
persons. The first revised draft was criticized and revised once more. The
process was repeated until there were seven revised drafts in all before the
programme was finally adopted unanimously by the full conference.

The same process of consultation was used in the election of the Central
People's Government Council, which is the permanent government of the
new People's Republic until the Political Consultative Conference meets again
in three years' time.

The various political parties and public organizations first made nomi-
nations to the Communist Party's United Front Department (established to

foster co-operation between the various democratic parties), which then compiled a nomination list. This list was submitted to the various groups for discussion and review. After two such reviews, the revised list went to the Presidium of the conference (a broad representative group of 89 members) for final revision before the list of candidates was printed. A secret vote was then taken. There was only one list of candidates, but it had been subject to thorough examination and revision. In addition, each voter was free to substitute names of his own for those appearing on the ballot. A majority of votes cast was required for election.

One of the Shanghai delegates said that a question frequently put to him, especially by foreigners, was about the role of the Communist Party in the new government. Friends had warned him, he said, that the Communists had great skill in gaining the support of people such as him, and then once having gained this support, taking away all freedom.

'My only answer,' he said, 'is that the leadership of the Communist Party is voluntarily and heartily accepted by the people. We all realize that China could not have won this victory had it not been for the Communists. We do not expect to have the advantages introduced by the Communist Party without having the Communist Party itself. And if the strength of the Communists is built on the support of the people, then the logical conclusion is that Communists are not afraid of the people. If they are not afraid of the people, why should they then take away their freedom?'

'But it wasn't a question of Communists versus non-Communists,' said another delegate. 'That is not an issue in the new China. It is the Chinese people who have stood up.' He went on to recall the speech made by Madame Sun Yat-sen at the opening of the P P C C:

'The new China is a non-fissionable product. It is a mighty force in the hands of millions ... Let us dedicate ourselves to prevent the destruction of civilization and exert every ounce of our energy to assure that the common people of the world get their due from life. That is to say that our task does not end until every hovel has been rebuilt into a decent house; until the products of the earth can be purchased by all; until profits from factories will be returned in equal amount to efforts expended; and until each family can have complete medical care from the cradle to the grave. Only when these necessities are equally at hand for everyone, regardless of race, colour, creed and residence in the world, can we say that we have reached our goal. This then is a call to the colours of New China, of the new world. Friends, delegates: let us all proceed with our task of establishing an independent, democratic, strong and prosperous New China, and together with the peoples of the world bring about everlasting peace on earth.'

The Common Programme

The Common Programme is a vitally important document. It is a precise statement of the general policies of the present Government of China. It details the governmental machinery and military system of China; it outlines economic, cultural and educational policies; it outlines the Government's foreign policy and its policy towards national minorities. It states what shall be done and what shall not be done in the new China.

The Common Programme is divided into seven chapters, and each separate chapter throws considerable light on the nature of the new China and its future development.

(1) *On General Principles.* The general principles of the Common Programme are the principles of New Democracy. The first condition is that the People's Republic of China must abolish 'all prerogatives of imperialist countries in China'. The feudal system of land ownership is to be abolished and its place taken by a system of peasant land ownership. All 'bureaucratic capital' is to be confiscated by the state, but private property and all legitimate private investments in industry and commerce are to be protected.

The object of all measures is to develop a prosperous economy and 'steadily transform China from an agrarian into an industrial country'.

There is a definite quality of dictatorship expressed in the policy of the new Chinese Government. The term used is 'people's democratic dictatorship'. The population is even divided into two categories: 'people', who have full political rights; and a small category who are deprived of political rights for a certain period although they are obliged to pay taxes and perform military service.

The 'people' are the working class, peasantry, middle classes, national capitalists and 'certain patriotic democratic elements who have come to awareness and crossed over from the reactionary class'. It should be explained that a national capitalist is any industrial or commercial employer who is not a bureaucratic capitalist.

Only feudal landlords and bureaucratic capitalists have no political rights—until they prove themselves useful citizens. Indolent feudal landlords are not to be confused with 'rich peasants' who may rent some land but who also till the soil. Bureaucratic capitalists, a very rare but extremely odious species, are the leading and responsible members of the four most reactionary Kuomintang cliques, the political economic groupings of Chiang Kai-shek, T. V. Soong, H. H. Kung and the Chens.

There is no mention made in the general principles of the Common Programme of socialism or communism. From various reports it is apparent that some delegates argued for the inclusion of 'socialism' as an aim of the P P C C. The argument was opposed by the Communist leaders. This was the reason given by Liu Shao-chi, speaking for the Communist Party: 'The Communist Party of China will support the P P C C and struggle for the realization of the Common Programme because it comprises the minimum programme of the Communist Party. The immediate policy of the Communist Party is to realize completely this minimum programme... But it is known to all that the Communist Party of China has, in addition to its minimum programme, its maximum programme, which is not included in the Common Programme of the P P C C. In the course of consultation, some delegates proposed to write down the future of socialism into the Common Programme, but we deem this to be inappropriate, because the taking of each serious socialist measure in China is a thing of the rather far future ... Without a doubt the future China will travel towards socialism and communism, because the outcome of the industrialization of China will either lead to socialism or turn China into an imperialist country. The latter alternative will not be allowed by the Chinese people or by the peoples of the world. But these are things of the far future, and they may very well be discussed by the P P C C in the future. The taking of socialist steps in China must be based on the actual needs of the social and economic development of China and on the demands of the majority of the people throughout the country. At that time, the Communist Party will certainly consult and make decisions jointly with the democratic parties and groups, people's organizations, national minorities and patriotic democratic personages.'

The statement makes it quite plain that the Communist Party, in 'the rather far future', is going to try to persuade the Chinese people to adopt full socialism. In the meantime it will concentrate on carrying out the minimum programme embodied in the policies of the P P C C.

(2) *Organs of State Power.* Under the chapter on Organs of State Power, reference is made to an All-China People's Congress that will be elected through universal suffrage, and to people's congresses at a lower level, also to be elected by universal suffrage. In the meantime, 'pending the convocation of the All-China People's Congress, elected through universal suffrage, the plenary session of the P P C C shall exercise the functions and powers of the All-China People's Congress'. When this All-China People's Congress does come into being, the P P C C will continue to exist as an advisory body.

Democracy is being systematically extended throughout China. Lack of familiarity with democratic processes and general illiteracy slow down progress, but the first steps toward eventual country-wide elections have been taken in the calling of hundreds of city, rural and regional people's representative conferences, small-scale replicas of the P P CC, their membership made up of delegates from peasant associations, trade unions, garrison troops, educational authorities, democratic parties and so on.

These nominated local conferences will gradually evolve into 'people's congresses' elected by universal suffrage and with powers to elect local and regional government organs. In some cities of the north-east, which have been liberated for several years, the local people's representative conferences already elect municipal governments and exercise the powers of people's congresses.

The movement is spreading through China from north to south. A Shanghai people's conference has already met several times, acting as an advisory and consultative body on municipal affairs. In rural areas, of course, local conferences turn their attention to such matters as flood control, afforestation and rent reduction.

How many years it will be before national general elections can be held no-one knows; but if the bulk of China progresses at the speed of the northeast, the national testing-ground, an All-China People's Congress may not be long delayed. No-one has been greatly surprised that the Western parliamentary system is not being adopted in China. Social and economic conditions have created the need for a method of representation and administration that is something like a soviet system, although not identical with that extant in the Soviet Union. China's democracy will develop according to China's needs.

(3) *Military System*. Among directives for the establishment of a modernized army, navy and air force under a unified command, there is the very important Article 24: 'The armed forces of the People's Republic of China shall, during peace-time, systematically take part in agricultural and industrial production to assist in national construction work, provided that their military duties are not thereby hampered.'

In December, 1949, Mao Tse-tung, as chairman of the People's Revolutionary Military Committee, issued a directive to the P L A ordering its officers and men to engage in productive work. This directive has been carried out throughout China, and a large number of China's five million soldiers are now engaged in land reclamation, agriculture, public works, fisheries and co-operative industries. Commercial transactions are strictly prohibited; but 40 per cent of the proceeds of productive work go to the troops engaged, and 60 per cent is divided into three equal parts—one for reinvestment, one for the army's daily expenses and the third for payment of taxes.

(4) *Economic Policy*. The chapter on Economic Policy is the largest and most detailed section of the Common Programme. The subject of People's Livelihood is regarded as the crucial issue for China. Everything turns on the

degree to which the Chinese people and their Government can 'overcome all difficulties' in restoring the tired, war-wrecked industry and agriculture of their country. This must be done. But it must be done in an entirely new way. The economy cannot be put together as it was before. A new pattern, new objectives have to be envisaged.

The new pattern is complicated, but the central direction of policy is stated in Article 21: 'Agrarian reform is the essential condition for the development of the productive forces and the industrialization of the country ...' In the new economy state and private interests will pull together towards a common objective, the industrialization of China. China is to be transformed into a modern industrial state. The Industrial Revolution, that disruptive blast from the West that broke the imperial dynasties, has at last claimed China as a home and now becomes a beneficial force.

(5) *Cultural and Educational Policy*. In passing we may note: 'national sports shall be promoted'; 'outstanding works of literature and the arts shall be encouraged and rewarded'; 'scientific knowledge shall be popularized'.

(6) *Policy Towards Nationalities*. There are several national minorities within the boundaries of China, and the Moslem communities of the northwest have always been treated with special care and attention by the Communists. The policy stated is: 'Regional autonomy shall be carried out in areas where national minorities are congregated ...' It seems that national minorities will be gently handled by the new Government, given full representation and 'have the freedom to develop their dialects and languages, to preserve or reform their customs, habits and religious beliefs'. The latest information on land reform suggests that this may be delayed in areas inhabited predominantly by national minorities.

(7) *Foreign Policy*. While every statement made by the Chinese Communists and the new Central People's Government affirms an alliance 'first of all with the Soviet Union' and the people's democracies of Eastern Europe, the Common Programme states that China will establish diplomatic and trade relations with all countries 'on the basis of equality, mutual benefit and mutual respect for territory and sovereignty'.

The total aspects of this fundamental policy and its consequences for Britain and the world will be considered in a later chapter. But, as with every policy of the Chinese P P C C and the Central People's Government, there is no confusion of intent. There has been a revolution in China, and China is now master of its fate. This is reported to the world.

Shanghai Celebrates

On October 10 Shanghai celebrated the founding of the People's Republic of China. Holiday was made.

I wandered through the streets, jostled by processions, deafened by the sounds of drums, cymbals, gongs, singing, trumpets, shouting of slogans, clapping, cheering and delighted laughter. A roar of applause for the appearance of a mighty dragon, rearing its fiercesome head with electric eyes; a surge and flow of people rushing to see each new sensation.

Picasso's peace dove, six-feet high, competing with paper aeroplanes, cotton-mill machines on poles, and monstrous paper engines. Parade after parade converged on the centre of the city, with the blue-gowned housewives the heroines of the day. Close behind came the street-sweepers with their brooms; and the silk-shop workers' union playing the 'International' on fifes and drums; carpenters, students, doctors, seamstresses and the makers of nails. One million people marching. They carried banners: 'Protect World Peace,' 'Long Live the People's Government,' 'Mao Tse-tung: Ten Thousand Years.'

Troops of schoolboys hurried to their meeting-places, flags aloft, loaves of bread sticking from their pockets. Flocks of 'whistling' pigeons whirled overhead. The beggar-children at the bridges shouted with excitement, blocking the streets with circular *yangko* dances of their own.

The dancers: girls in wine-red and blue. Drum-sticks and stamping feet. Then four men, with abacus, tea-kettle, broom, and fish, dancing. The comedy of the oyster and the crab; the slow measures of the peasant and plough, the daughter sowing seed; and then again, the great rearing dragon carried by a hundred men.

All day and all night long; lanterns and blazing rockets; steamers hooting on the river. China shouting its approval.

Chapter Seven

LAND TO THE TILLER

B ASIC, primary, in China's revolution is agrarian reform. The 'impact' of revolution is four hundred million peasants reaching out for land.

I have drawn attention to the complexity of China's old economy, to the fact that 'traditional Chinese industry is suffuse among the villages, and ... that the farmers depend upon it for subsistence.' I also noted that the penetration of the Industrial Revolution shattered this whole complex village self-sufficiency. This penetration has been in part responsible for China's present compelling need to industrialize her economy; and its effects have greatly aggravated the hunger for land.

But the land problem always existed in China. It was *inherent* in the old feudal economy. Western economic penetration merely accelerated the need for reform, and added acute political complications. The feudal economy was not only inefficient; it was extremely unjust and oppressive. China's inner history has been the long struggle of a tormented peasantry fighting for livelihood, justice and land. But the peasants have had to wait until the twentieth century for a decision.

How has the land been divided? A conservative estimate, based on the considerable research that has been done, reveals that the landlords, who made up only 4 per cent of the rural population, owned 51 per cent of the cultivated land; and the rich peasants, who made up 6 per cent of the population, owned 18 per cent of the land. In other words, about 10 per cent of the rural population owned together 69 per cent of all cultivated land.

The second fact revealed is that, while tenant rentals vary from district to district, they are found in general to be never less than 50 per cent of the yield of the land; and in some cases as much as 70 to 80 per cent of the yield.

Behind these facts and figures is the real crux of China's land problem.

Landlordism carried with it definite social rights in China, sanctioned by custom, religion and law. The landlord was protected by Heaven and the Confucian analects. The poor farmer, caught in a maze of superstitions, was out of favour with the Gods. Flood, blight, all natural calamities, descended upon him as mystic forces of nature beyond the control of man.

The landlords were the feudal rulers. The biggest of them were always the local officials, and, either openly or secretly, they exempted themselves from all civic obligations. Taxes, 'contributions', conscription and other services were eventually passed on to the poor peasant, the tenant farmers and the day labourers. About them the landlords gathered personal soldiery and local 'bullies' who were the agents of their authority.

Power was accumulative. In addition to high land rentals, the landlords often exacted from their tenants payments in kind and labour services. And as often as not the landlords were the local usurers. To pay the landlord the peasant borrowed from the landlord. At every turn of the screw, the landlords acquired more of the earth and the peasants sank deeper into poverty.

This system has continued right down to the present day, its injustice and sheer inefficiency intensified by foreign imperialism, war-lord plundering and Kuomintang corruption.

No wonder that when the reckoning comes the accusations are bitter. Here is an extract from the account of an Accusation Meeting held at Shuanghuaishu, near Peking, where liberated peasants were settling accounts with their worst landlord, one Kuan Chang-sheng (Ever-victorious Kuan):

As soon as Ko Lin stopped speaking an old woman pushed through the crowd and pointed her finger directly at Kuan. 'Black-hearted Kuan!

You took our five *mow** of land, Kuan. Is it not true? And when my starving husband fell ill, Kuan, you told the Japanese he had an infectious disease and they burned him alive. True or not, Kuan? My husband's brother could not make a living because of your persecution and he finally hanged himself. Is it not true, Kuan?'

Another woman thrust herself forward, tears streaming down her face: 'You took our land just before harvest and kept our crops as well. You threw my son in jail and offered him up to the Japanese devils for their army. Where is my son now? Give my son back to me now...'

(If the reader is anxious about the fate of Ever-victorious Kuan, it is recorded that after this meeting a local court sentenced him to four years' imprisonment.)

Go to the Country

In Shanghai last year a young member of the Rural Service Corps talked about two months he spent in the south studying the problems of the land and the lessons of the momentous beginnings of land reform.

'I remember,' he said, 'when I first walked out of the gate of the walled city the paddy fields spread out around me like green satin ... It was in the afternoon that I arrived at Lientan. It is near the Changshu county of south Kiangsu. There are small rivers winding through the fields and big lakes nearby as reservoirs. But all I saw was sorrow and desolation. Why? Because of the flood, the flood! The land is high there, but the dikes were destroyed by Chiang's bandits when they built their fortifications. So the storm brought the waters into the fields and over the houses. Well, a flood may go down in time but the houses are destroyed and the grain seed ruined. How could the peasants keep themselves alive in the endless days to come?

'The call came to fight the disaster. In every district emergency committees were formed with the positive elements leading. The Rural Service Corps members were mobilized and went to the countryside.

---

* *One-sixth of an acre.*

'I saw with my own eyes how they ran through the deep flooded fields under the scorching sun and amid cloudbursts. They worked with the peasants in building emergency dikes and mobilizing all pumps. They persuaded the pessimists to stand up and fight against nature. They called on the selfish whose fields were not yet flooded to join in the emergency work. They convinced all that by working together they could overcome all difficulties.

'And so I learned—*We must go to the country*!

'And then I learned—*Study the people*!

'In Lientan the Rural Service Corps members had this conviction: to learn from the people, to learn from the masses. The best discussion meeting of all was held on the open ground near Cheng Hwang Temple. The members analysed the character of the peasants: their virtues of hard work, endurance and strength in love and hate; and their shortsightedness and ignorance of over-all interests. They concluded that the correct policy was to help the peasants to "break through their old thinking". The peasants do not easily accept new thoughts, but when they do they stick to the very end.

'Then we must—*Arouse the people*!

'When two boats carrying our members arrived at Chi Chia Hsiang the farmers were dumbfounded. Never before had men in uniform come to "live" with them. The women hurried away to hide their benches, tables and buckets lest the men in uniform "borrow" them. The young boys ran about trying to see what was going to happen.

'The members walked into the village and sat down to rest, singing. Some of them began to chat to those peasants who were brave enough to stand near them. Some encouraged the young boys to sing.

'Gradually the members and the peasants became friends, and, at last, they were "one big family". The women were no longer afraid and they left their benches outside the houses. Then the peasants would tell us of their sufferings under reactionary rule. Only those who have seen them, talked with them and, above all, lived with them can understand the misery of those long and dark days.

'Widow Hsi, with tears in her eyes, told the members how she paid a sum equal to several *piculs* of rice to save her only son from "conscription". But the reactionaries put his name back on the list. She had no more grain or money and so he had to flee and live in the open fields until liberation. Old Mr and Mrs Wang were both over sixty years of age, yet they were asked to pay the tax "for able-bodied men". When they refused they were unmercifully beaten until they changed their minds. And still they were squeezed by the landlord. The peasants would sing:

> Sun rises red,
> Moon rises yellow,
> We all love life
> But work to the grave.
> Sore backs, heads swimming,
> No rice to bring home.

'When the news about the arrest of the former chief of the town, Mr Pan, was passed to the villages, the peasants were overjoyed. "Who would arrest this damned *tsengchang* if not the Communists? Liquidate him! Where and how did he get his dirty money? That bloodsucker!" Then their anger exploded: "Come on! Take him down to the villages. Let each of us bite him once and then kill him."

'Then I learned—*A fair distribution of burdens*!

'It wasn't easy to mobilize the peasants to discharge their duty and pay the next tax for the summer season.

'It is clear that the landlords never paid in the past and that the poorest suffered. The new tax of the People's Government is different. The members talk it over with the peasants themselves and fix a tax in kind. They lighten the burden on the poor, the widows and the families of martyrs. There must be no extra taxes whatsoever.

'But there were no slight difficulties. It is policy that the peasants should pay their due willingly and positively instead of by compulsion. But some took a "wait and see" attitude, while a few fooled us by pretending to be "very revolutionary". But the poor were gradually awakened. They stood behind the members.

'Tang Ah-ping was a poor peasant with only one *mow* of land, and there was his old mother. At the peasant conference on tax distribution all agreed that he should be fully exempt. But he refused. "The People's Government is for the poor," he said. "I have twenty-five *catties** of seed left over. I will contribute a share." The story of this happening spread to all the villages. The support of the poorest peasants is our greatest strength.

'Then I learned—*The weeds must be cleared away*!

'The landlords and their "bullies" were always waiting for their chance. In the far-off villages where the members had not been, the peasants asked such questions as: "Has Shanghai already been liberated?" Here was the reactionaries opportunity. They told the peasants: "Chiang Kai-shek will come back to eat his moon-cake at the mid-autumn festival." When our members came to these villages they were unwelcome. The peasants were selling their chickens and ducks as cheaply as pork. They had been told that the People's Government would tax all their possessions even after taking the tax in kind! But we started the peasant associations. The poor began to awaken. Then the reactionary agents spread the rumour: "The Communists ask you to join the peasant associations which are actually stations for army recruits. If you join up you will be taken away."

'But at last the people were not frightened. The landlords were forced out into the open and all could see their intrigues. Their agents were exposed.

'The peasants began to cry out—*The weeds must be cleared from the grain*!

'When I went back to the walled city everything was beginning to change. The peasants smiled at us in all the villages.'

The Higher Policy

This one man's experiences reflected what was but the very beginning of the land reform movement in one small area. When the Communists first began an agrarian reform movement in earnest in 1927 they redivided the

---

*1 catty = 1¹/₃ lb; 100 catties = 1 picul.

land equally among all. Over the years they learned the grave weaknesses of this approach, especially its neglect of the 'middle-class' farmer. From 1933 they began to think in terms of landlords, rich peasants, middle and poor peasants, and farm labourers; and they were far more successful. During the anti-Japanese war, as we have noted, they suspended land confiscation altogether and adopted a milder policy of rent and interest reduction, a very considerable concession made in the interests of broad national unity. This policy they maintained until the outbreak of civil war in 1946.

When intense and bitter fighting spread from the northeast in 1946 the Communist Party reintroduced land confiscation, although the policy directives of the Party's Central Committee forbade the seizure of the land of rich peasants, and, of course, of the middle peasants.

But the Central Committee's directives could not be carried out. The Communist rank and file in the countryside and the masses of the peasants went ahead on their own, followed their own needs and instincts, and confiscated both landlord and rich peasant land, goods and property. The rich peasants were 'leaning to the side' of the landlords and the Kuomintang: the poor peasants were shouldering the immense burdens of the Liberation war. Yet the peasantry needed to be fired with a revolutionary enthusiasm, and if there had not been an extremely thorough agrarian reform, satisfying the needs and demands of the poor peasantry, the Liberation war effort would have been considerably weakened. The Communist leadership did make strong efforts to correct excesses and to bring order into a rather chaotic economic situation, but they had to accept in general the anti-rich peasant line. So bitter was the struggle that, it seems, no other policy could have succeeded.

The situation in 1950 is considerably different. The war on the mainland has been virtually completed. The peasantry have no longer to contribute military service and public labour. The amount of 'public grain' collected from them is much lighter. While the Central People's Government regards the fight for Taiwan (Formosa) as a 'huge task', the army is said to have enough strength to shoulder it. The chief problem now is the restoration, reform and development of the national economy. It is the solution of *eco-*

nomic problems that determines the form of the agrarian reform policy of today.

Discussing the total economic and social implications of land reform in 1950, Liu Shao-chi says in a most significant statement: 'Our views of the basic reason for and aim of agrarian reform is different from the view that agrarian reform is only designed to relieve the poor people. The Communist Party has always fought for the interests of the labouring poor, but the ideas of Communists have always been different from those of philanthropists. The results of agrarian reform are beneficial to the impoverished labouring peasants. They can help peasants partly solve the question of their poverty. But the basic aim of agrarian reform is not purely one of relieving poor peasants. It is designed to set free the rural productive forces, that is, to free rural labourers, land and other means of production from the shackles of the feudal ownership system of the landlord class, in order to develop agricultural production and to clear the path for the industrialization of China. The question of poverty among the peasantry can be finally solved only if agricultural production can be greatly developed, if the industrialization of New China can be realized, if the living standards of the people throughout the country can be raised, and if China finally proceeds upon the road of socialist development. By merely carrying out agrarian reform, part, but not all, of the problem of the peasant's poverty can be solved.'*

The Communists are not 'philanthropists'. They have a large and comprehensive view of China's present needs and future possible development. As builders they are prepared to use every available material for their purpose, and they will sink deep foundations for their new society. No doubt the Communist Party played a considerable part in drafting the new Agrarian Reform Law of the People's Republic of China, adopted by the Central People's Government Council on June 28, 1950.

---

* *Liu Shao-chi, now a Vice-Chairman of the People's Republic, in a report to the Second Session of the National Committee of the P P C C held in Peking, June, 1950.*

Agrarian Reform Today

Article 1 of the new agrarian law reads: 'The land ownership system of feudal exploitation by the landlord class shall be abolished, and the system of peasant land ownership shall be carried into effect in order to set free the rural productive forces, develop agricultural production and pave the way for the industrialization of the new China.'

Article 2 reads: 'The land, draught animals, farm implements and surplus grain of the landlords and their surplus houses in the countryside shall be confiscated, but their other properties shall not be confiscated.'

Article 4 reads: '... Industrial and commercial enterprises run by landlords and the land and other properties used directly by landlords for the operation of commercial and industrial enterprises shall not be confiscated...'

Article 6: 'Land owned by rich peasants and cultivated by them or by hired labour, and their other properties, shall be protected from infringement ...'

Article 7: 'Land and other properties of middle peasants (including well-to-do middle peasants) shall be protected from infringement.'

Article 10: 'All confiscated or requisitioned land and other means of production, with the exception of those to be nationalized as provided by this law, shall be taken over by the *hsiang** peasant associations for distribution in a unified, equitable and rational manner to poor peasants with little or no land and to those who lack other means of production. Landlords shall be given an equal share so that they can rely on their own labour and reform themselves through labour.'

In all there are forty Articles to the Agrarian Reform Law. Those given above deal with the major aspects of the Law. The rich peasant employers of labour are to be protected and encouraged. Clearly evident is the central aim of increased production, not simply for agriculture but for the whole economy. Even landlords are permitted to keep industrial and commercial enterprises, because 'according to past experience, if these properties of the landlords are

---

* *A hsiang is an administrative unit embracing several villages.*

confiscated and distributed ... chaotic conditions can easily arise, and wastage and destruction of great quantities of social wealth will also occur.' Beyond this it would seem that the Law encourages those with wealth to turn to industry and commerce, sharply reversing the retrogressive tendency of former days when the wealthy put their money into land as the best security.

The Law is remarkable for its clarity and common sense. One notes that the 'tillers' (poor peasants who have had a little property) will receive from confiscated land a slightly greater allocation than former landless peasants. 'The tillers will be happy because the land they rented from others now becomes their own, there is no need to pay rent or to humble themselves before the landlords, their social status is raised, the land they acquire is more than others and they are better off.' Also, special land allotments are insisted upon for the families of martyrs who lost their lives in the various revolutions from 1911 and the anti-Japanese war.

The peasants are called upon to secure the help of all who support agrarian reform, intellectuals, village school-teachers and 'enlightened gentry'. The peasant associations are required to pay attention to recruiting the womenfolk of peasant families as association members, and to encourage women to take leading positions in the associations and local governments. Monks, nuns, taoists and priests and refugee landlords who have fled from other areas in the past are to be given shares of land and other means of production similar to the peasants', 'otherwise they will become jobless vagrants, upset public order and be very injurious to the interests of the people'.

There is a twofold purpose. Economically, production is to be increased: politically, the old feudal society is to be uprooted, new social forces set free and the basis laid for a better, more rational society.

What Has Been Done

Agrarian reform was completed in the north-east by March, 1949, and extended down into north China and Honan province last winter.

In the extensive newly-liberated areas the initial work of rounding up Kuomintang soldiers and bandits, disarming landlord agents, carrying out rent reduction and establishing peasant associations was undertaken by local authorities, the People's Liberation Army and Rural Service Corps. According to reports from east and central-south China, some 24 million peasants joined peasant associations in these areas, over 38,000 *hsiang* governments were re-formed, and numerous peasants' and people's representative conferences convened.

At present, agrarian reform in China has been completed, or practically completed, in an area with a rural population of about 145 millions (total population of the area is about 160 millions). There are still areas with a rural population of about 264 millions (total population of about 310 millions) where agrarian reform has not been carried out. In these remaining areas reform will be extended by several yearly stages following autumn harvests.

Meanwhile, large irrigation and construction projects have been started from one end of China to the other. Work is in progress on a national plan aimed primarily at flood control but also at extending the country's irrigation systems and improving the network of internal waterways.

In north Kiangsu and north Anhwei alone more than one million peasants have been engaged in heightening and broadening the dikes along the Yangtse and the Hwai rivers and in cutting mammoth canals to divert the courses of various small rivers and streams. North of the Yangtse to the coast 250,000 men are cutting a canal through which the Yi River will flow across the flat plain of north Kiangsu into the Yellow Sea. The completion of this canal (200 kilometres long) will bring close to 2,500,000 acres of flood-devastated land permanently under cultivation. The cost of this canal is set at 100,000 tons of grain; but the yearly crop expected from the reclaimed land is estimated at more than 300,000 tons.

A great many People's Liberation Army troops are taking part in these and other projects, and reports state that large numbers of volunteers from the cities, including groups of medical workers, school-teachers and students have gone out to provide medical care and to establish schools for the construction workers.

An immediate stimulus to agricultural production is the issue by regional governments of cheap credits to farmers and direct loans in the form of large quantities of grain seeds. On a national level, the burden of taxation is being altered in favour of the countryside as against the cities. 'Public grain' still makes up 37.2 per cent of the national budget, but last year's assessments on the various regional areas are reported to have been met in the main, with the north-east and the north-west surpassing their quotas.

The level of agricultural production for the whole of China at the beginning of 1950 was still 25 per cent below the 1936 pre-war level. In some newly-liberated areas production was as much as $33^1/_3$ per cent below the pre-war norm. In the older liberated areas of the north, in spite of considerable progress, production was still about 14 per cent below pre-war.

China must not only reach pre-war levels of agricultural production, but she must also go far beyond pre-war levels to achieve self-sufficiency in foodstuffs and cotton.

Further, the People's Government has undertaken to restore at least part of the traditional village industry of China. Although in time industrialization will overcome the need for dispersed, miniscule village crafts, there will be a long interim period during which every possible source of production must be tapped. In some areas long monopolized by Western or Japanese commerce the peasants will actually have to be taught their old craft techniques again. In this aspect of rural production new producers and marketing co-operatives will play a tremendous role.

If there were no other problem in China but that of restoring and developing agricultural production, the new Government would face a task that would dismay all but the most confident. But no palliatives are proposed. There is no appeal to world charity. The People's Government relies upon the resources of China, the industry and skill of a freed people and rational planning.

The new Agrarian Reform Law of the People's Republic can provide a practical basis for a revived agriculture. It is meant to do so for many years to come. According to Liu Shao-chi: 'The policy adopted by us of preserving a rich peasant economy is, of course, not a temporary but a long-term policy.

That is to say, a rich peasant economy will be preserved in the whole stage of New Democracy. Only when the conditions mature for the wide use of mechanical farming, for the organization of collective farms and for the Socialist reform of the rural areas can the need for a rich peasant economy cease, and this will take a somewhat lengthy time to achieve.'

Chapter Eight

LABOUR, CAPITAL AND THE STATE

THE People's Liberation Army came into the city, bringing happiness and freedom. The people's army, the liberator of those who toil, had taken charge. In the city the workers stood up and shouted: 'No longer shall we be slaves!' And the sound of this shouting came to the ears of Old Chang, who worked in the office of Manager Tsao, sweeping the floors, bringing tea, watching the door at night. 'Ah!' said Old Chang. 'Our army has arrived. The old life is finished. I shan't slave for *laopan* Tsao any longer!' And he threw his broom into the corner and refused to bring any tea.

Manager Tsao was much distressed when a representative of the People's Government came making inquiries about the affairs of the company. Manager Tsao did not want to complain about Old Chang but he felt obliged to describe the situation. When he had finished speaking and the representative of the People's Government was about to reply, Old Chang stepped forward: 'Comrade representative!' he said. 'Now that we workers are liberated, I propose that Manager Tsao be made to sweep his own floor.'

The representative of the People's Govermnent thought about this for some time. Finally be picked up the broom from the corner where Old Chang had thrown it and gave it to Manager Tsao. 'Very well,' he said, 'Manager Tsao can sweep the floor.'

Old Chang was delighted. Then the representative turned to him and said: 'Comrade Chang, you see that Manager Tsao is sweeping the floor. Now I propose that you sit at Manager Tsao's desk.'

Old Chang was somewhat surprised and not a little embarrassed to be seated in the leather chair. Before him were sheafs of receipts, orders and figures, and a high stack of ledgers. Then the representative said: 'Comrade Chang, please bring the accounts of the company right up to date and give me a full statement of the present financial position. The People's Government has asked me to ascertain the nature and extent of the company's business.' Old Chang blinked in amazement, and the representative continued: 'Of course, we cannot allow any mistakes or omissions, Comrade, and we will hold you personally responsible for each error and deficiency.'

'But,' said Old Chang, 'Aiya! I am the doorman-sweeper, Comrade representative. I can even cook. But as for figures ... Do not torture me, Comrade!'

'Then,' said the representative, 'in the meantime you may go on with the sweeping, Comrade, and Manager Tsao can deal with the accounts. Agreed?'

The representative of the People's Government smiled, and both Manager Tsao and Old Chang gladly assented to his proposal.

This simple fable is one of several that the People's Government propagandists brought with them to Shanghai. In it they summed up the policy of the new Government on worker-employer relationships under New Democracy. For those more interested in the theoretical approach, they stated that the policy meant 'taking into account both public and private interests, benefits to both labour and capital'.

Big and Little Fish

In the first days of Shanghai's liberation there was much confusion and mismanagement. True, a core of politically-organised trade unionists had done much to prepare for liberation, had protected factories, assisted the P L A and immediately restored production. These were the dockyard, power station and public utility workers generally. But they were but a part of the whole.

The majority of Shanghai's proletariat was unorganized or held membership of bogus Kuomintang unions or of labour gangs. These labour gangs were well entrenched in China's cities, closely linked with old feudal societies, criminal groups and superstitious associations. Transport workers in the major cities could only obtain work through gaining membership of one gang or another, and this meant paying a large portion of earnings to the gang leader and his minions. The saying was: 'Big fish eat little fish; little fish eat shrimps; shrimps eat mud.' The worker was the shrimp.

Feuds and violence were common between rival gangs and within the gangs themselves. The biggest gang leaders kept their own private guards and held private courts at which they tried and brutally punished recalcitrant members. Their's was a highly profitable business and they guarded it ferociously. All this led to gross inefficiency and exorbitant transport charges. I have been told by the managing agent of a large foreign shipping firm that his company had to pay a regular salary to the gang leader on their wharf in order to get any loading or unloading done at all.

After the liberation of Shanghai and other cities the People's Government could not easily uproot the long-established practices of the gangs. Some of the richest gangsters had fled to Taiwan, Hong Kong and the United States, but the great majority remained. The workers were still under their thumb, terrorized by threats and rumours that Chiang Kai-shek would return. Some gang leaders outwardly made a rapid adjustment to the new situation. Chen Hao-chu, one of Shanghai's leading underworld figures, transformed his gang of 3,000 men into a fake dockers' union two days after liberation. So terrorized were these men that it was some time before the authorities could find out the truth of the situation. When they did, no quarter was given. The ordinary workers in the gang were encouraged to denounce Chen Hao-chu and list his crimes against them. Chen was tried on a capital charge and shot. His lieutenants were, however, treated leniently and several other gang leaders were persuaded to break up their organizations and throw themselves on the mercy of the People's Government.

Takeover officials themselves were not entirely free from mistakes in their handling of the situation. Often they attempted to proceed too quickly, bullied workers into new trade unions and ended up as unpopular as many of the old officials. Some workers spontaneously made exorbitant demands on manufacturers, who were unable to pay higher wages, or even meet normal wage commitments, because of the chaotic state of the market. New officials, their sympathies naturally with the workers, found it difficult to check this spontaneous movement. Others went to the opposite extreme and alienated the workers by brusquely dismissing all complaints.

Commercial and industrial employers were uncertain about the whole position. The times were most painful for foreign businessmen, who had no one to appeal to and who were fair game for unruly elements who imagined they could win any concession under the guise of 'anti-imperialism'. And, of course, it was difficult for foremen and overseers in foreign companies to accept the fact that they could no longer physically assault or dismiss workers with impunity.

Not until August, when a 'Provisional Procedure for Mediating and Settling Labour-Capital Disputes' was issued by the Military Control Commission, was some order restored. These regulations stated that when worker-employer disputes occurred the employer was not permitted to cease production or to stop payment of wages, and the workers were not permitted to obstruct production or break labour discipline. Employers were permitted to discharge workers according to the needs of production, but were required to pay a 'termination' allowance of one to three months' wages.

The procedure for mediating worker-employer disputes was that, first of all, both parties should strive for a reasonable solution through consultation and collective agreement. If this failed, both parties or either party could appeal to the Shanghai Labour Bureau for mediation. If mediation failed, the Bureau was legally entitled to arbitrate the dispute. If both workers and employers, or either party, were dissatisfied with the arbitration of the Labour Bureau, the case could be referred to the People's Court.

Shanghai presented perhaps the most difficult problem in 1949. In China's north-east conditions in the large industrial centres were stabilized and a major part of the industry state-owned. Some large enterprises in Shanghai, the property of the Kuomintang or of the Four Big Families, were nationalized after the takeover, but many of the large factories and mills, and nearly all the thousands of small concerns, remained in private hands according to law. The need for trade unions was certainly not abolished.

Li Li-san*, speaking at a W F T U conference in Peking, November 12, 1949, spoke of the wage system in China as follows: 'Under the democratic government the wage system in state enterprises is based on the principles of "pay according to work done", and "more work, more pay". We oppose equalitarianism and adopt various methods and systems of awards to encourage technical progress and labour initiative. At the same time, we guarantee the workers' minimum living standard, and couple the improvement of workers' livelihood with the development of production.'

Since April of this year there has been a marked improvement in Shanghai and central-south China. Stabilization of the national economy, resumption of town-country trade and fuller employment have smoothed out many problems. The Trade Union Law of the People's Republic, promulgated on July 16, 1950, has made worker-management relations in state industry, and worker-employer relations in private industry, a good deal clearer. In both cases, increased production is the ultimate test for settling all differences of opinion. Yet it is plain that the working class, through its trade unions, is to be given a special and responsible status under New Democracy.

The new Trade Union Law specifies that the trade unions have the right to take part in the administration of state-operated concerns, and the right to sign collective agreements in private concerns. The trade unions have rights of investigation into the hiring and firing of employees in all enterprises. Unions are voluntary organizations partly financed by membership dues and Government subsidy. But, in addition, management and owners of factories,

---

* Minister of Labour in the Central People's Government.

mines, shops, schools and other productive or administrative concerns are required to allocate to their local trade union organization each month, as trade union funds, a sum equal to 2 per cent of the total amount of monthly wages.'

The People's Government and the Chinese Communists intend to make the trade unions strong and influential, the 'pillars' of the New Democracy.

The Leading Class

The Chinese Communists have always considered themselves to be thorough-going Marxists, and one must take this into account when studying their policies and their terminology. They interpret national and international politics in the terms of class struggle, class relationships and class power. They regard political parties (their own included) as but the articulate and organized expression of class interests. Thus the Chinese Communist Party regards itself as the party of the Chinese working class, though simultaneously representative of the peasantry as the closest 'ally' of the working class.

Where class ends and party begins is not readily deduced without constant practice of the dialectic; but the Communists insist that, while they are at the throttle, the working class is the engine of the Chinese revolution. An added difficulty is that the Chinese Communists have been frequently designated as 'agrarian reformers' or 'national revolutionaries'. They would admit to being such, but would again insist that they are first and foremost a party of the Chinese proletariat, a party of the 'world proletarian Socialist revolution'.

They point to the fact that the Chinese Communist Party came into being hard upon the victory of the October revolution in Russia and with the appearance of an industrial proletariat in China. In the early 1920s the Communists devoted most of their energies to the organization of revolutionary trade unions, and since then they have held undisputed leadership of the genuine trade union movements of China.

The personal progress of Liu Shao-chi is a case-history in point. He was born in Ninghsiang county of Hunan in 1900. He was a student when he became a foundation member of the Communist Party in 1921. He was the first president of the famous Anyuan Trade Union of Kiangsu, one of the first miners' unions, noted for its strength and militancy. He was an organizer of the first national trade union congress and became vice-chairman of the All-China Federation of Labour when it was founded in 1925. Driven underground in 1927, he continued to direct the illegal trade union movement until 1932. Then he joined Mao Tse-tung in the Soviet area of Kiangsu, as did so many other leaders and rank-and-file trade unionists forced to flee from the city terror. From that time Liu Shao-chi continued his association with the trade union movement and became one of the highest Communist Party functionaries. Today he is Honorary President of the All-China Federation of Labour as well as a Vice-Chairman of the Central People's Government.

Although, throughout their history, the Communists have relied upon the quantitative strength of the peasantry, they have always regarded the organized revolutionary trade unionists as the nucleus and most reliable section of their movement. This may help clarify Article 1 of the Common Programme of the P P PC, which reads: 'The People's Republic of China is a State of New Democracy, that is, People's Democracy. This Republic carries out the People's Democratic Dictatorship led by the working class, based on the alliance of workers and peasants, and rallying all the democratic classes and nationalities in China.'

Mao Tse-tung puts the case for the workers in his *People's Democratic Dictatorship*, published on July 1, 1949: 'The people's democratic dictatorship needs the leadership of the working class, because only the working class is very far-sighted, just, unselfish and endowed with revolutionary thoroughness. The history of the entire Chinese revolution proves that without the leadership of the working class the revolution is bound to fail, and with the leadership of the working class the revolution is victorious. In the era of imperialism no other class in any country can lead any genuine revolution to victory. This is clearly proved by the fact that the Chinese petty bourgeoisie and national bourgeoisie led the revolution many times and failed.'

Then Mao Tse-tung continues. 'The national bourgeoisie is of great importance at this present stage. Imperialism is still standing near us and this enemy is very fierce. A long time is required for China to realize true economic independence. Only when China's industries are developed, and China no longer depends upon foreign countries economically, can there be real complete independence. The proportion of China's modern industry in the entire national economy is still very small. There are, as yet, no reliable figures, but according to certain data it is estimated that modern industrial production makes up only about 10 per cent of the total productive output of the whole national economy. To cope with imperialist oppression and to raise our backward economic status one step higher, China must utilize all urban and rural capitalist forces which are beneficial and not detrimental to the national economy of New Democracy, and unite with the national bourgeoisie in common struggle. Our present policy is to restrict capital but not to eliminate it...'

State and Private Enterprise

The policy of restricting capital has not meant reducing the quantity of capital in private hands (if we discount the possessions of the Four Big Families). Restriction has meant keeping the control of the national economy in the hands of the state. Within the sectors marked off for it, private capital is encouraged to go forth and multiply.

The Common Programme declares that the People's Government 'shall encourage the active operation of all private economic enterprises beneficial to national welfare and people's livelihood and foster their development'. The continual stress on the word *beneficial* does not imply any hindrance of private enterprise. One can restrict the flow of a river in order to channel it into power turbines. Capital in China has so often been used in the past for pure speculation, for unproductive and harmful commercial practices. Shanghai's economic life in the last years of the Kuomintang was rotten with speculative and black-market dealing on a grand scale. Dozens of fly-by-night banks and bogus companies existed simply to exploit market changes, political upheavals and natural calamities. It was nothing to buy and sell a stock of rice ten times over and thereby make a small fortune.

All emphasis is now on the productive employment of capital. The speculators and the Yellow Ox Gang are out of business. The gold and silver shops of Shanghai now display books, shoes, sewing-machines. New industries and private merchants are both encouraged, but capital is restricted in a fashion beneficial to the national economy. It cannot be used for speculation, and the state control of certain industries and over-all control of domestic and foreign trade means that private capital can be encouraged to flow into state enterprises. Article 31 of the Common Programme states: 'The economy of co-operation between state and private capital is of a state-capitalist nature. Whenever necessary and possible private capital shall be encouraged to de-velop along the direction of state-capitalism, for example, producing for state-owned enterprises, operating jointly with the state, or operating state-owned enterprises and exploiting the state-owned resources through the form of concessions.'

For some time, in Shanghai at least, Government controls were open to criticism. The takeover officials who were required to investigate industry and commerce were very suspicious of private businessmen and lacked ex-perience of practical economics. There were annoying delays while officials learned elementary lessons and lost some of their distrust.

They did learn in the end, but complaints against them were in any case minor compared with the criticism of the first taxation schemes. It had hardly been the custom in Shanghai for the wealthy to pay taxes at all: when they were over-assessed by Communists it was almost the end of the world. However, serious criticism of the taxation was that, as markets dried up in the initial period, taxes that might have been met by legitimate enterprises in normal circumstances became instead an extremely severe burden.

The New Democracy has had economic growing pains. The Government and its officials made mistakes. Yet one realizes that foresight as well as stubbornness dictates the radically new conceptions of China's economic development. (Radically new in the sense that they are the first application of

Sun Yat-sen's principle of Nationalism to China's economy.) The People's Government is determined, for example, to alter completely the economic character of Shanghai. It intends to cut Shanghai's binding ties with foreign-owned capital, and to integrate the city into a new national economy. Shanghai will, in future, look inwards. Some of its industry will be shifted nearer to sources of native raw materials, domestic markets and power resources throughout China.

Military defence will also be a consideration. The repeated bombing of Shanghai by Chiang Kai-shek's Taiwan-based aircraft is not forgotten. Workers and employers remember the raid of February 6, 1950, when the Shanghai Power Company was so heavily damaged that two-thirds of the city's industry was put out of action. Then a year of Chiang's naval blockade, with the disruption and unemployment it engendered, showed up Shanghai's dependence on foreign ties and enabled the People's Government to give workers and businessmen an object-lesson in the dangers of having too much to do with 'foreign imperialism'.

What is remarkable is that Shanghai and the newly-liberated areas of central-south China have reached relative stability in a year of revolution, blockade, bombing and natural disasters. The most recent reports from Shanghai indicate that commodity prices have maintained a steady downward trend since April, that employment is up and that many industries are back on their feet. Private capital now has its claims more fully met, policies are more flexible, taxation more reasonable, and industries that have been through months of continual losses have begun to show a profit again. Communications, especially railways, have been thoroughly restored and now operate expeditiously. Production and trade is expanding. *The Times*, London, September 22, 1950, quotes reports that the volume of exports from Hong Kong to China for the first eight months of this year showed a 120 per cent increase over the same months of last year.

The Ruhr of China

Mao Tse-tung is able to say, without running counter to the principles of

New Democracy: 'In China there is no excess of domestic capitalism. On the contrary our capitalism is too small.' China's national capitalists hold only some 30 per cent of the total industrial capital investment, and this total is meagre. In 1936 (from the last available figures) China's industrial capital investment per capita was $5 compared with the $1,600 of the United States. Industrially China is extremely backward.

The one sector where there is the beginnings of a modern heavy industry is in north-east China (Manchuria). Here an industrial base near copious natural resources was developed by the Japanese, and this industry has now been taken over by the state. In the north-east there are considerable quantities of coal, iron, dolomite, magnesite, aluminous shale, structural and chemical raw materials, gold and subordinate amounts of silver, copper, lead, zinc, tungsten and less important metals. The total possible coal reserve is esti-mated at a figure of 9,000,000,000 tons. And the north-east is also a rich agricultural area. In 1943, under the Japanese, the industrial north-east pro-duced 87 per cent of the nation's total pig-iron output, 93 per cent of the finished steel products, 40 per cent of the coal, and 78 per cent of the electric power. Japan used the north-east to reinforce her war machine: today, con-trol of this Ruhr of China gives the Central People's Government command of China's national economic development.

At the time of the takeover the north-east economy was in very bad shape. In August, 1948, fighting, looting and sheer neglect had left not a single bridge standing, coal-pits flooded, many factories levelled to the ground and skilled factory workers dispersed. The iron-smelting works of today still have only 25 per cent of the equipment that existed under the Japanese. A good deal of machinery and plant had been broken up, sold or destroyed by the Kuomintang. Some had been acquired as war booty much earlier by the Soviet army and taken to the Soviet Union.

Nevertheless, progress has been substantial. The north-east regional People's Government balanced its budget in 1949 and, at the same time, provided the P L A with the essential supplies needed for its southern campaigns. In 1949 the north-east produced 500,000 tons of surplus grain; a million new workers entered state-owned industry; and, according to the *New China News Agency*, real wages rose 27 per cent. Over half 1950's budget expenditure by the regional government was marked for heavy industrial development. The peak 1943 production level is expected to be reached by 1953; and, by that time, agricultural production will have surpassed the previous highest level.

Soviet Assistance

Not a little of the progress is due to aid and assistance received from the Soviet Union. Barter agreements with the north-east regional government in 1948-49 provided that area with Soviet industrial equipment, vehicles, petroleum, textiles, paper and pharmaceuticals. In return, the north-east delivered soya beans, vegetable oil, maize and rice.

Of the two hundred Soviet industrial and transport experts who went to China in 1949, the majority were directed by the Chinese Government to work in north-east China. In Dairen and Port Arthur alone Soviet experts are reported to have trained 14,000 Chinese workers as technicians and engineers, and 115 as factory manager-administrators. The Russians are instructors; but they have been of considerable direct assistance in the restoration and development of railways and the restoration of industrial potential. These Soviet experts have come for a limited period, and they invariably work under Chinese direction and accept the same salary and conditions as Chinese of equal rank and authority. It would appear that they have made a favourable impression upon the majority of Chinese with whom they have come in contact. I talked to a young Chinese executive from the new north-east rubber industry that is receiving Soviet technical assistance. He said of the Russians: 'They are mostly older men, forty years of age and over. They are really above the grade of engineers. Many speak English and German. They are very patient. They demonstrate everything with their hands. They explain everything three times.'

Of even greater importance to China's reconstruction is the Sino-Soviet agreement on the Granting of Credits to the People's Republic of China, signed on February 14, 1950.

Article 1 of the agreement reads: 'The Government of the Union of Socialist Soviet Republics grants the Central People's Government of China credit, counting in dollars, amounting to 300 million American dollars, taking 35 American dollars for one ounce of pure gold.

'In view of the extreme devastation of China as a result of prolonged hostilities on its territory, the Soviet Government has agreed to grant credit on favourable terms with 1 per cent annual interest.'

It is stipulated in the agreement that this credit, to be used in five equal portions over five years, will cover the purchase of equipment and materials including the equipment for electric power stations, metallurgical and engineering plants, equipment for mines for the production of coal and ores, railway and other transport materials. It will be repaid with deliveries of raw materials, tea, gold, American dollars, in ten yearly parts between December, 1954, and December, 1963. The Soviet Government agreed at the same time to hand over gratis to the Chinese Central People's Government the property acquired by the Soviet army from Japanese owners in Manchuria.

A Sino-Soviet agreement has also been signed for the mutual exploitation of the oil deposits of Sinkiang, the far western province of China. From these possibly vast resources China in recent years has produced less oil annually than the British Isles have done. Soviet machines and technicians will, of necessity, play the major part in a great extension of the existing fields. But China and the Soviet Union will share equally in the resulting production, and the new industry, over three-yearly periods, will be alternately under Soviet and Chinese direction.

An opinion voiced in certain quarters is that the very generosity of the published Soviet agreements with China indicates that there must be secret clauses disadvantageous to China. But the Chinese laugh at this idea. One is reminded that, in 1938-39, the Soviet Union extended barter credits amounting to $250,000,000 to the then Nationalist Government. They explain that the new agreements indicate that the Soviet Union maintains its traditional attitude of extending aid and assistance to any strong Chinese central government that is willing and able to defend the sovereignty and integrity of China.

Chapter Nine

THE MIND AND THE HEART

CHINA is being rebuilt, transformed. Above all, the builders of the new China are transforming themselves. The children of the Yellow Emperor are becoming a new people.

The Shanghai *Giefang Rhbao* (Liberation Daily) published this first lesson in a new latinization of the 3,000-year-old Chinese character writing. I have added an English translation:

Di-I Ko (Lesson 1)

1. Womn sh Zhungguorhen (We are Chinese).
2. Ni sh Zhungguorhen (You are Chinese).
3. Taie sh Zhungguorhen (He is also Chinese).
4. Womn du sh Zhungguorhen (We are also Chinese).
5. Zhungguorhen du ai Zhungguo (Chinese all love China).
6. Ni sh Zhungguorhen ma? (Are you Chinese?).
7. Shd, wo sh Zhungguorhen (Yes, I am Chinese).
8. Ta ne? Taie sh Zhungguorhen (He? He is also Chinese).
9. Ni bu ai Zhungguo ma? (Do you not love China?).
10. Womn duai Zhungguo (We all love China).

In several ways this is a first lesson, in a new writing *and* in the cultural and educational rebuilding of China. For the Common Programme of the P P

C C declares: 'Love for the fatherland and the people, love of labour, love of science and the taking care of public property shall be promoted as the public spirit of all nationals of the People's Republic of China.'

Quite deliberately, at every opportunity, a new ethics of citizenship is being instilled into the Chinese people. Many years ago the Communists learned the crucial value of civic discipline and morality for all who strive to win the leadership of the Chinese people, a people whose traditional philosophy has been based on ethical systems rather than upon religious faith. The ethics that the Communists preach today they themselves have practised for many years.

Those who saw the men of the P L A entering Shanghai were forcibly impressed by what one might call their *virtue*. This quality came not by chance. It had been taught, learned and practised, not only by the troops that entered Shanghai but by the whole Communist army.

Here is a set of directives issued by headquarters to P L A troops before they entered north west China, which is predominantly a Moslem area:

1. Protect the mosques and Moslem priests. Do not enter religious places, and never put up posters or drawings on the walls of mosques.

2. Never eat pig, horse or mule meat in Moslem houses.

3. Never make advances to young Moslem women nor enter their homes.

4. Do not disturb religious services.

5. Do not wash in Moslem bath-houses.

6. Wash your hands before drawing water from the wells of Moslems. Do not pour water back into the wells.

7. Address Moslems as *Lao Hsiang* (old fellow-countryman) or *Lao Piao* (old cousin), but never as *Hui Tse* (a rude term for Moslems).

8. Never mention pigs before Moslems. Do not ask them why they don't eat pork or what mosques are for.

9. Never drink or smoke in Moslem homes.

10. Tell everyone about the party's policy toward the national

minorities.

Here is practical virtue, with a purpose. But the question arises: although the behaviour of the Communists may be acceptable, what of their over-all beliefs and purpose? What are the real social 'ends and means' of the Chinese Communists?

From an original source, Mao Tse-tung: 'As for love of mankind, there has been no such all-embracing love since society was divided into classes. The ruling class has preached universal love. Confucius advocated it, so did Tolstoy. But no one has ever been able to practise it because it cannot be attained in a class society.

'A true love of mankind is attainable, but only in the future when class distinctions have been eliminated throughout the world. Classes serve to divide society: when classes are eliminated society will be united again. At that time the love of mankind will flourish, but it cannot flourish now. Today we cannot love the fascists nor can we love our enemies. We cannot love all that is evil and ugly in society. It is our object to eliminate all these evils.'*

The purpose is not left in doubt. The Communists intend to eliminate all which they believe is evil in society. Virtue for them lies only in action.

Half as Useful as an Ox

The first national law to be adopted by the Central People's Government—before even the Agrarian or the Trade Union Laws—was the Marriage Law of the People's Republic of China, promulgated on May 1, 1950, after seventeen months of study and preparation.

This law is designed to help eradicate once and for all the most detestable feature of the old Chinese society, the feudal subjugation of women. On the women of China all evils fell twice. If the men of China were oppressed by feudal society, then the women were oppressed by both the society and the men.

Women were chattels in the old society. In Nanking, even after liberation, there was a case reported of a pedicab-driver who came to the people's court

---

* From an address to cultural workers, Yenan, May 23, 1942.

complaining that he had sold his wife for a sack of white rice and that the buyer had not paid up in full! In Honan, a few months before liberation, a widow was beaten to death by village elders for trying to re-marry. In Hofei, Anhwei Province, it was found that in one village of 281 families only 22 families had no child bride living with them. The young girls sold into marriage faced a life of most cruel exploitation. All such things were common.

The new Marriage Law strikes at the root of the subjugation of women. It reads, 'Article 1: The arbitrary and compulsory feudal marriage system, which is based on the superiority of man over woman and ignores the children's interests, is abolished.

'The New Democratic marriage system, which is based on free choice of partners, on monogamy, on equal rights for both sexes, and on protection of the lawful interests of women and children, shall be put into effect.

'Article 2: Polygamy, concubinage, child betrothal, interference with the re-marriage of widows and the exaction of money or gifts in connection with marriage shall be prohibited.' Persons violating the law will be punished.

The women of China are to be guaranteed equal rights with men in marriage and in political, economic, cultural, educational and social life. And they are to be organized to see that they get these rights. The first All-China Women's Congress opened in Peking in April, 1949. Here, for the first time in history, women of China gathered together to consider their problems and their future. They met under silken banners in the throne room of the old Imperial Palace. But they were not pampered darlings of the rich: they were those 'half as useful as an ox, if not quite as helpful as a hired hand.' They were cotton-mill operatives, guerilla fighters and peasant mothers. Among them was delegate Liu Ching-ying, aged 32, and already a grandmother with a married son 18 years old. There was Cheng Li-hung, a girl from Tsingtao, who told a correspondent: 'A friend of mine worked up to two days before she died of tuberculosis. She had a family to support. She would mix bean husks with corn to stop her hunger, and her stomach was huge although her arms were just bone. Her family had no money for a coffin and we workers found the wood.'

The women workers of China have suffered a double exploitation. Now it is recognized that to drive out the evils of the past the women must have new and basic economic rights. Slavery, polygamy, concubinage and prostitution will be finally wiped out when women, universally, can find suitable productive work and receive for their work the same wages as men. New laws and better conditions go hand in hand.

The change is being made. The length of the working day for women has been shortened, no woman may work in unsuitable trades, and, as far as possible, night work is avoided. Leave on full pay for confinement is 45 days, with a shorter rest for miscarriage. Equal pay for equal work is being introduced. On the land, for the first time in history, land title deeds are being issued to women without discrimination.

The women's congress in Peking, the formation of special women's federations, the election of Madame Sun Yat-sen and many other women to higher positions in the Government, together with the new Marriage Law, will do much to guarantee that the New Democracy shall be for all. A most detested evil is being struck down.

Coal to the Snowbound

Perhaps the next greatest social evil in China is illiteracy. Well over 80 per cent of the population can neither read nor write. This is an enormous block to progress; and it is doubtful that there can be a modern, unified, democratic, industrialized China until a majority of the adult population is literate and educated. In his speech to the cultural workers in Yenan, Mao Tse-tung said: 'Our primary duty to them (workers, peasants and soldiers) is not to "add flowers to embroidery" but to "send coal to the snowbound". Our first and foremost concern must be to educate rather than to try to raise the standard. It would be wrong for us to underestimate or overlook the work of education.'

Again north-east China, the older liberated area, leads in the campaign against illiteracy. Practically the whole adult populations of Port Arthur and Dairen have participated in study since liberation, in working hours, at night schools, in their homes and at study groups. Illiteracy is disappearing.

The city of Dairen's 'model student' is one Hsieh Shih-shan, 35 years old, who was once an illiterate coolie in the refrigerating department of the Dairen Fishing Corporation.

Hsieh Shih-shan now knows 1,400 characters (of the traditional and still current Chinese script) and has been elected manager of his department. Hsieh studied characters and mechanical engineering at the same time: he 'rode two horses at once'. At work he increased production, held a trade union position and taught his fellow-workers; and at his home he studied, although his wife was wont to throw his blackboard out of the window. Hsieh Shih-shan received the title of Dairen 'Study Model' because of his outstanding diligence in combining his studies with his work.

The Chinese peasants are as eager to learn as the workers in the cities. He who is literate is an honoured man. In the slack winter season millions of peasant farmers, men and women, form themselves into study groups. With the help of those who have been to school, of students from the cities and of Communist cadres, they meet during the long evenings for instruction and practice. Special readers are issued for beginners and there are many newspapers printed in a simplified style with a restricted vocabulary. As the peasant students progress they produce wall-newspapers of their own. It is noted that once the womenfolk 'break through' their old fears and restrictions they are among the most ardent supporters of the anti-illiteracy campaign.

At the beginning of this chapter I quoted a first lesson in *Latinxua*, a latinization of the Chinese written language, a new phonetic script using the familiar latin letters and designed to replace or supplement the old character writing. To learn the old traditional script, the Chinese student must memorize thousands of complicated characters instead of the mere 26 letters of the latin alphabet. Chinese printers cannot use linotype machines for the traditional script; books and newspapers must be set by hand from a fount of over 6,000 characters; telegrams must be sent by a numeral system; catalogues, card indexes and dictionaries become a complicated maze.

Undoubtedly a latin alphabet and a phonetic script will have to be introduced into modern China: industrialization will be difficult without it. At present the most popular candidate for the honour is the above-quoted *Latinxua* (pronounced 'latin-hwar'), which was developed in Moscow in 1928 by a Chinese Communist, Chu Ch'iu-pei. Last year a Chinese Language Reform Association was established to 'find a system for the latinization of the Chinese language and to simplify the Chinese characters'. No latinization is yet officially supported by the Government, and there is loud and bitter opposition, particularly from the well-read intelligentsia, whose cultural superiority would be reduced, they imagine, by the introduction of a new simple script. But much official encouragement is being given to the language reform movement, and I believe that latinization will be systematically introduced in the not too distant future.

From Objective Facts

All progress in the new China is a struggle, a battle against feudal tradition, illiteracy, class privilege. There are those who could lead, but who do not wish to get their hands dirty: there are those who should lead, but who are tongue-tied. The weight of ancient prejudice is not easily shifted.

The Chinese Communists realize that if social progress is to be thorough, it must be slow. Issuing decrees will settle nothing: each individual must be convinced that every change is desirable: each individual must prepare himself to carry out every necessary change. Logic and objective thinking, the ability to change, the willingness to criticize and to accept criticism, these are required of the citizen of New China.

A new attitude to life, the moulding of the new citizen, is described by a Canadian professor in Chengtu's West China Union University: 'One special technique which the Communists have brought is now widely used: group criticism. For instance, in the Department of Education one evening they took the student department officers of the last term and dealt with them one by one. The one in question would first say where he or she thought he had failed in his work for that office. Then everyone in the group would bring up good points and bad points about him. Some of them he would regard as unfair and would give his reasons. Others he would acknowledge at once were fair criticisms. Occasionally a criticism would be based on personal prejudice and at once someone else would point out the fact. When attitudes were not objective, it would be noted and stressed that "truth can be arrived at only from objective facts". That is one of the main points of Marx's dialectical materialism, which is now on everyone's lips. The amazing thing is that the individual criticized does not seem to have his feelings hurt! Since all are regarding him objectively, he is helped to look "objectively" at himself. Surely that is the basic attitude of the Christian!'*

Whatever the attitude is, whether it is Marxist or Christian, a great change is in progress in China, a revolution that reaches from top to bottom of society, a revolution of mind and heart, a revolution that affects and concerns each institution and every individual in that vast land.

A change in the nature of one-fourth of humanity cannot but be of consequence for us all.

* China Weekly Review. *Shanghai, April 8, 1950.*

Chapter Ten

CHINA AND THE WORLD

'It is the pattern of Oriental psychology to respect and follow aggressive, resolute aud dynamic leadership...?

General Douglas MacArthur.

TODAY, China has five million men under arms. The core of this army is a group of battle-seasoned officers and men who have been in action continually for very many years. China is on the road to becoming an industrialized nation. In time she will be able to build tanks, heavy artillery and bombers. Even now her army is being mechanized and greatly strengthened. She is building up a modern air force and a navy. Add to this that Mao Tse-tung is noted not only for his writings on literature and art, but also for his 'brilliant theories and rich experiences' of war. And that China is strongly united under its present leaders. And that there are four hundred and seventy-five million Chinese. Then add to all this the proposition: 'It is the pattern of Oriental psychology to respect and follow aggressive, resolute and dynamic leadership...'*

And what follows?

'The lustful thrusts of those who stand for slavery as against liberty, for atheism against God.'* A larger Pearl Harbour? A China following in the

---

* Both quoted from General MacArthur's address to the Veterans of Foreign Wars. (Time, September 4, 1950.)

100

footsteps of Japanese imperialism? A 'dynamic' China, like Genghis Khan, bending its bows against the eagles of the Pacific and the West? An eastern Armageddon?

Why not? Is it not logical?

To tell the truth, the idea had never occurred to me before I read General MacArthur's psychological opinion. Now I have been forced to think back on the last year in China to search for details and possible evidence I may have missed. Can I have entirely overlooked the extraordinary prospect of an imperialist China?

There was one incident. It was during Shanghai's parades and carnival in celebration of the founding of the new Republic. I had been wandering among the crowds, deafened and somewhat exhausted, and had come to a halt where Nanking Road joins the Bund. Passing at the moment was a troop of costumed workers dancing a comic mime. They had a villainous Uncle Sam leading a battered Chiang Kai-shek on a leash, and a lesser John Bull and General de Gaulle all prancing about a spinning coloured globe. They were riotously making fun of the West.

A ragged coolie noticed me watching the play and touched my elbow: '*Wai kuo jen*,' he said, '*Ti kuo chu i!* (Foreigner. Imperialism!)' And he turned, grinning with amusement, to his companions. They nodded at me, their eyes sparkling: '*I ting ti! Ti kuo chu i!* (Certainly! Imperialism!)' They were all vastly amused, and yet they were concerned about my feelings, that I might misunderstand the meaning of the play. I had to smile with them.

The images set up as the enemies of China were symbols of colonialism, of imperialism. Toward a flesh-and-blood foreigner there was no animosity. Anti-foreignism is ruled out of the propaganda of the new China, and the man-in-the-street knows it.

But, of course, it is not as simple as that. I have met Chinese who could not even bear to hear the sound of Japanese being spoken. Memories of the brutal and sometimes fiendish behaviour of Japanese police, soldiers and airmen are still ingrained in many ordinary people. It certainly cannot be said that all Chinese are quite free from anti-foreign feeling.

Does this mean that China wants war? From experience I would say that it strengthens the desire for peace. I recall the favourite English phrase of my Chinese teacher, a mother of three children, who had seen much of the horrors of war and of Japanese imperialism. She had been separated from her family, driven across China, seen Japan's disastrous adventure run its course. Her oft-repeated phrase was: 'Whom the gods are about to destroy, they first make mad.' And she would conclude: 'Those who are thinking of another war now are already insane.'

I have been looking through my 'Brandt', my old lesson book, and have come across these three phrases which my teacher added because they were coming into everyday use; 'Everyone must learn to criticise and accept criticism the period of New Democracy will last for some time the people of all countries want peace.' She believed that these phrases should be drummed in.

Well, I have been trying to recollect evidence of Chinese imperialism, but the evidence is eluding me. All I can find is anti-war and anti-imperialist propaganda.

Perhaps the streets and the homes of Chinese people are the wrong quarters in which to look for imperialism. It can be assumed that the people of all countries want peace and are against colonial conquest. What of governments, and of the Chinese Communists? To refer back to Liu Shao-chi's report on the Common Programme: 'Without a doubt, the future of China will travel towards socialism and communism, because the outcome of the industrialization of China will either lead to socialism *or turn China into an imperialist country. The latter alternative will not be allowed by the Chinese people and the people of the world.*'

We face then what is, according to Liu Shao-chi (and Mao Tse-tung), the other alternative: a future socialist and communist China. But it must be left to the reader to decide whether or not this suggestion of the future elimination of capitalism in China constitutes an act of aggression against the United States and the West. At least, a communist China is a matter of 'the far future', and there are much more pressing and immediate issues.

On August 1 this year, the 23rd anniversary of the Chinese People's Liberation Army, its commander-in-chief, Chu Teh, made this statement: 'Our war of liberation is not yet concluded. We have still to liberate Taiwan and Tibet. On June 27 President Truman suddenly ordered the American Navy to prevent us from liberating Taiwan. This is, of course, aggression against China by the United States. It must be pointed out that this is entirely unlawful; even the United States Government itself has not discovered any 'legal grounds' for this act of aggression...

I find no evidence to show that China does not intend to do more than 'liberate all the territory of the country and fulfil the great cause of unifying China,' but there is not the shadow of a doubt that China will seek to regain Taiwan (i.e. Formosa) and Tibet, by force of arms if all other means fail.

Tibet and Taiwan

The Chinese Central People's Government regards Tibet as an integral part of China. (I have noticed that the world map in the Piccadilly Underground, like all standard maps, does likewise.) In fact, Tibet is a virtually autonomous frontier province over which China has exercised nominal sovereignty. Britain has had considerable influence in Tibet since the Younghusband expedition to Lhasa in 1904; but no Chinese government has recognized this British influence as legal.

On July 8, 1949, the Tibetan authorities expelled the Kuomintang government personnel from Tibet, the explanation being that this would prevent the province from becoming involved in the civil war. In 1950 representatives of the Tibetan authorities left Lhasa to conduct negotiations on the invitation of the Chinese Central People's Government.

Reports from China quoted P L A General Liu Po-cheng, at a meeting of the South-west Military and Administrative Council in August, 1950, as stating: 'The P L A will soon advance into Tibet.' He added that Tibet will be granted regional autonomy, that freedom of religious belief will be ensured, the Tibetan language fostered, educational facilities extended and economic reforms introduced. Former 'pro-Kuomintang and pro-imperialist officials' will not be punished and will retain their respective posts if they 'sever all relations with the reactionaries and do not engage in sabotage'. All the expenses of the P L A units entering Tibet will be borne by the Central People's Government.

But this problem is now insignificant beside the issue of Taiwan (Formosa). Here is 'strange eruption' indeed. Here is a debate foreshadowing a conflict ten times more dangerous than in Korea, Indo-China, Malaya, all combined.

Taiwan is an island, in size slightly larger than Holland, about 100 miles from the coast of China. Chinese settlement began in the thirteenth century. From the end of the seventeenth century immigration from the mainland provinces of Fukien and Kwangtung steadily increased. Today there is a total Chinese population of some 6,500,000 speaking the Fukien dialect, and 170,000 people of national minorities.

Taiwan became part of the Chinese Empire in 1683. In the latter half of the nineteenth century, as we have noted, all the great powers were staking claims on Chinese soil. Japan attacked China in 1894; the weak Manchu Government was defeated and ceded Taiwan (and the Liaotung peninsula) in 1895. The Taiwanese people did not recognize this capitulation and fought the Japanese invaders, continuing their resistance for a number of years. The Japanese held on, and their rule became what has been called 'a model of colonial exploitation' (*Time*, September 11, 1950).

Following upon the May 4 Movement in China, in 1919, there was a rebirth of the anti-Japanese movement on Taiwan. Foremost among the new Taiwanese 'liberationists' was Hsieh Hsueh-hung, a Taiwanese woman who studied at Shanghai University in the mid-1920s and returned to her home country to participate in underground activities. She was caught by the Japanese in 1931 and imprisoned for nine years. She survived various Japanese barbarities and lived to see their defeat, only to have a price put on her head by the Kuomintang for her leadership of the independence movement that almost won the island in February, 1947. Today she is chairman of the Taiwan Democratic Self-Government League and a member of the Presidium of the Chinese P P C C in Peking. The presence of Hsieh Hsueh-hung in the councils of the Central People's Government is taken to indicate that this Government will grant Taiwan a measure of home rule when it disposes of the Kuomintang remnants who are still in possession of the island.

Japan held Taiwan until VJ Day. The Cairo Declaration, signed in December, 1943, in the name of Britain, the United States and China, had stated: 'All the territories that Japan has stolen from the Chinese, such as Manchuria, Formosa and the Pescadores, shall be restored to the Republic of China.' This decision was confirmed at the Potsdam Conference, and the island (with Manchuria and the Pescadores) reverted to China after the surrender of Japan. Taiwan was taken over by Chiang Kai-shek and the Kuomintang.

The record of Chiang Kai-shek's administration in Taiwan need not be reviewed. It is a record of corruption and violence. Observers have described it as worse (if that were possible) than his administration on the mainland,

The problem is that to this day, although the Kuomintang has lost all semblance of authority on the mainland and the Chinese people give their allegiance to the Central People's Government, Chiang Kai-shek still retains Taiwan. It is the last vestige of his power in China and his last 'qualification' to represent China in the councils of the United Nations Organization. From Taiwan, Chiang Kai-shek can and does direct hostilities against the mainland. Without a doubt he dreams of revenge and a return, although it is reported that 'hopes of returning to the mainland have been deferred even by Chiang Kai-shek himself to a date at least three years hence' (*The Times*, September 27, 1950).

Obviously the Central People's Government seeks to drive Chiang Kai-shek's forces into the sea, and Chiang Kai-shek himself into final oblivion. Few Chinese would oppose this, and 'there the matter would end, were it not that many member governments of the United Nations still regard Chiang Kai-shek as the legal representative of the Chinese people, and that some of these governments continue to give moral, economic and military aid to the remnants of the Kuomintang forces on Taiwan.

The most charitable view of the action of those governments who still recognize Chiang Kai-shek as the representative of the Chinese people is that their action is based on misinformation about the state of affairs in China. But those who render aid to Chiang's remnant Kuomintang forces should realize that they have put themselves in the line of fire in the last act of China's war of liberation. They are leaving themselves fully exposed to the danger of becoming involved in a war not only with the Chinese People's Liberation Army, but with at least four hundred and fifty million Chinese.

China in Asia

The Central People's Government is adamant in its intention to bring Taiwan and Tibet under its authority. Will it go beyond? That is, when Taiwan and Tibet are recovered, will the People's Liberation Army stop at that?

There has been no public suggestion of aggressive intent on the part of the Chinese Government, and I heard no private rumour of it in China. Indeed, such a suggestion would be bitterly resented in China, and mark one out as either an ignoramus or a provocateur.

Where China's political sympathies and interests lie is another matter. It should be remembered that the People's Republic of China has recognized the Vietnam Government of Ho Chi-minh and the North Korean People's Government, and has established diplomatic and trade relations with them.

France and the United States may well regard this as an unfriendly attitude. No doubt the Chinese Government looks upon the presence near its borders of troops from France and the United States (neither of which recognizes it) as equally unfriendly. And the action of the United States forces in planting the Kuomintang flag ashore at Inchon in Korea, some 100 miles from the frontier of China's north-east, is hardly calculated to change the Chinese Government's policy of recognizing North Korea. While warfare and unrest continue in Korea and indo-China, and while neither France nor the United States nor the United Nations as a whole recognizes the Chinese Government, the situation will remain tense and 'incidents' are bound to ring louder than may seem warranted.

Further afield, the People's Republic of China has made clear its intentions. It will vigorously defend the status of Chinese communities abroad, and as an Asian nation it regards all movements for self-determination among Asian peoples as worthy of support. In November, 1949, a trade union conference of Asian countries met in Peking. At this conference delegate Luu Duc Pho of Vietnam is reported to have said: 'The oppressed nations of south-east Asia are closely linked with China historically, geographically, culturally and socially. The victory of the Chinese people is of decisive importance for the nations of south-east Asia.' This is a common sentiment in China. As Britain sees herself as part of a European community, so the Chinese see themselves in the larger setting of Asia. What happens anywhere in Asia touches the Chinese; every advance in China stimulates the Asian peoples. Any attack or threat of attack upon the territory of nations in Asia is a threat to China.

The foreign policy of the People's Republic of China is based on the principle of 'safeguarding independence, freedom and integrity of the territory and sovereignty of the country, support of international lasting peace and friendly co-operation between peoples of all countries, and the opposing of the imperialist policy of aggression and war' (Article 54, the Common Programme).

The main application of this foreign policy is an alliance with Soviet Russia against the revival of an aggressive Japan *'or states allied with it'*. The protection of north-east China (Manchuria) may well provide the key to her policy.

Three times in this century Japan has launched attacks through Korea and the north directed simultaneously at China and Russia. The Russo-Japanese War (1904-05) was fought in China's north-east and involved the seizure of Chinese territory. In 1918 Japanese forces led the intervention against the young Soviet state in Siberia; and during the nineteen-twenties Japan continued, by intrigue, military pressure and the weapon of assassination, to attempt the annexation of the whole of the north-east. When these adventures failed, Japan attacked and seized the north-east in 1931 and established there the puppet state of Manchukuo, from which it launched its campaigns against the bulk of China and its assaults against the Soviet Union at Changkuseng and in the Lake Khassan area.

Apart from ideological sympathies, China and the Soviet Union have an historic interest in common defence against Japan.

The Chinese do not consider that the menace of Japan has been removed by the Japanese surrender in 1945, or by the Allied occupation policy, which was criticized by even very conservative opinion in China well before the events of 1949. The 1948 Draper Mission* to Japan (described by the Japanese press as the beginnings of the restoration of Japan as 'a stabilizing influence in the Orient') was regarded with deep suspicion in China. Now that the 'democratization' of Japan has been halted, the *zaibatsu* industrial-financial oligarchy permitted to resume business, new measures taken to expand Japan's industrial potential, and the release of several batches of war criminals (many with shocking records in China) ordered by General MacArthur, China's suspicions have been increased.

The Chinese see danger in a *zaibatsu*, industrialized Japan as long as their own economy remains backward. And they fear the continued existence of the Japanese militarists. Memories of the frightful years of Japanese invasion are undiminished. Thus the Chinese reaction can well be imagined when it was publicly announced in Tokyo, in November, 1949, that Hiroshu Nemoto, one-time commander of the Japanese army in China, had been allowed to leave Japan and assist Chiang Kai-shek in the defence of Fukien province against the People's Liberation Army. The Chinese could not believe that General MacArthur's headquarters were ignorant of Nemoto's movements.

Nor are the Chinese likely to overlook the arrant challenge offered in such statements as that attributed to Major-General Chennault, saying that: 'America hasn't got enough people to win a war in China without Asian allies' (*Time*, September 18, 1950).

---

* *An American economic mission led by William H. Draper.*

To indicate the importance given in China to the problem of Japan, I quote four suggestions for a Peace Treaty with Japan as given in an influential Shanghai journal: '(a) In accordance with the Potsdam Conference decisions, the drafting of the Peace Treaty should be undertaken by China, the Soviet Union, the United States and Britain, the powers which made the greatest contributions in the war against Japan; (b) in accordance with the precedent established after the first world war when the peace conference was held in Paris, the capital of the most devastated country, the Peace Conference with Japan should take place in Peking; (c) only the eleven nations represented on the Far-Eastern Commission should participate in the actual conference; and (d) with reference to reparations, as China fought for the longest time and made the greatest sacrifices, at least 50 per cent of all reparations should go to China.'*

This is not a statement of official policy; but it is a measure of public opinion on the problem of Japan.

The official policy is expressed in the Sino-Soviet Treaty of Friendship, Alliance and Mutual Assistance signed on February 14, 1950. In this treaty China and the Soviet Union have made a firm and binding agreement to prevent 'the resumption of aggression and violation of peace on the part of Japan and any other state which would unite with Japan directly or in any other forms in acts of aggression.' If either China or the Soviet Union is attacked by Japan 'or states allied with it' they will render each other 'military and other assistance with all means at their disposal'.

If any state should use Japan as a base of operations against either China or the Soviet Union, there is little doubt as to how such action would be interpreted in the light of the Sino-Soviet Treaty.

China's treaty with the Soviet Union goes further than military defence. The two parties have agreed to 'develop and consolidate economic and cultural ties between China and the Soviet Union'. This, however, does not mean that either party will prejudice its own sovereignty in rendering the other

* World Culture, *Shanghai, November 18, 1949.*

economic aid. It is stated in Article 5 of the treaty that all relations shall be undertaken 'in the spirit of friendship and co-operation and in conformity with the principles of equality, mutual interest, and also mutual respect for state sovereignty and territorial integrity and non-interference in the internal affairs of the other party'.

It would appear then that China is determined to pursue the traditional policy of rejecting all interference by outside countries, without exception, in her internal affairs.

New China—Friend or Foe?

The present Chinese Government and the Chinese Communists do not expect to receive aid and encouragement from any source other than the Soviet Union and Eastern Europe. Mao Tse-tung writes: 'During his lifetime Sun Yat-sen many times appealed to imperialist countries for aid. The appeal was futile: instead he met with merciless attacks. In his lifetime Sun Yat-sen received international aid only once and that was from the U S S R.'* The present Chinese Government intends to 'lean to one side', to pursue a socialist and communist course within China, and to unite with the Soviet Union on international issues.

Does a substantial majority of the Chinese people who have considered the question agree with this policy? The answer is, in the light of past and present history, yes. Would these Chinese welcome closer relations with Britain? Again, yes. At the expense of the alliance with the Soviet Union? No. Do these Chinese consider friendly relations with the United States possible? No, not until the United States has severed relations with Chiang Kai-shek and recognized the Central People's Government. This is not mere acceptance of Government policy, but the logical thinking of all educated Chinese who support the Government. The number of those who do not is negligible.

The wish of the Chinese people and the intention of the Chinese Government is to pursue a policy of establishing diplomatic relations 'on the

---

* The People's Democratic Dictatorship, *July 1, 1949.*

basis of equality, mutual benefit and mutual respect for territory and sovereignty with foreign governments which sever relations with the Kuomintang reactionaries and adopt a friendly attitude to the People's Republic of China.'

Trade with foreign countries, 'on the basis of equality and mutual benefit', is also desired. According to the Shanghai *Ta Kung Pao* (January 11, 1950): 'It is completely agreeable to us that England is in favour of trade with China. Since in turning to a programme of peaceful reconstruction China will require large quantities of machinery, and in the implementation of agrarian reforms the broadest agricultural markets will be developed, the future of Sino-British trade will be bright.' The most recent reports from Hong Kong indicate that the new China is eager to exchange its foreign currency for any amount of British goods.

Unfortunately, the recognition of the Chinese Central People's Government as the *de jure* government of China by the British Government on January 6, 1950, was not followed up by an exchange of full diplomatic relations. On the one hand, Mr Bevin called the action an 'awkward decision'; on the other, a spokesman of the Chinese Ministry of Foreign Affairs suggested that Britain 'has not in reality completely severed its relationship with the remnant reactionary clique of the Kuomintang'. But when trade is extended between Britain and China, and there is no longer a 'clique of the Kuomintang' in existence on Taiwan and in the United Nations to confuse the issue, relations between the two countries should improve.

Is the new China, then, to be considered a friend or foe?

In the foreseeable future China will be fully occupied in the tasks of reconstruction and in fulfilling the tremendous projects which it has conceived. The land will have to be enriched, great new industries constructed, and the 'coal' of knowledge brought to the 'snowbound'. Another war can bring nothing but disaster to China's hopes and plans.

Certainly the people of China desire peace, and yet the issue of peace or conflict, for instance, between Britain and China, will not be settled by agreement between these two countries. Both are part of one world and their problems have become world problems. It rests with the United Nations Organisation, and upon its proper functioning and the justice of its decisions, to ensure that all questions of friendship between China and the rest of the world shall be peacefully decided.

And, first of all, the United Nations cannot function properly or hope to make just decisions while the People's Republic of China is unrepresented, while one-fourth of humanity is silenced. As Sir John Pratt, the experienced Far-Eastern diplomat, has written: 'So long as the United Nations continues to recognize Chiang Kai-shek and his associates now sheltering in Formosa as the Government of China many will continue to regard the Charter as a sham' (*The Times*, August 11, 1950).

At the Paris Peace Conference in January, 1919, Britain, the United States, France, Italy and Japan consulted together on the future of the world. At this conference Japan claimed right of succession to Germany's ill-gotten holdings in Shantung in China. And even though China had been an ally of these five powers in the Great War, China was not even consulted on the disposal of her territory. The reaction to this in China was the mighty May 4 Movement which united the Chinese people in the conviction that they had no hope of friendship from the West.

Similarly, if today any action is taken—on the Taiwan (Formosa) issue, on a Peace Treaty with Japan, or on any other problem of world consequence— by the United Nations Organization without the consultation and participation of the Chinese People's Republic, then this action will tend to create an irrevocable conflict between China and the West, between China and the United Nations, between Britain and China. It will also alienate a large section of the peoples of Asia, particularly in India.

Madame Sun Yat-sen, honoured Vice-Chairman of the Chinese Central People's Govermnent, has said of the future of the new China: 'Every shot fired to bring Taiwan back to its rightful owner, every step taken to liberate Tibet, means that much more security for the world. For upon completion of these tasks the people can devote full time and energy to the reconstruction of their country. We have known war in this land almost continuously for one hundred years. We are more than ready for peace. We demand it. The Chinese people want to make themselves a bigger bowl for more rice, and they want to contribute to the world's happiness at the same time.'

This is the voice of China, and it is the plan for the future. There is much to be done. China has not become a Utopia. The way ahead for the Chinese people will be arduous. But there is a saying in the new China: '*Tsou, tsou; ts'ou, ts'ou; kai, kai*! (Act, act; you will make mistakes; correct them, correct them!)'. It is in this spirit that the Chinese people will advance.

Their Chairman, Mao Tse-tung, has said: 'We have taken but one step in a 10,000 *li* march.'

图书在版编目（CIP）数据

新中国：朋友还是敌人／（新西兰）福尔克纳（Falconer, A.）著.
－北京：外文出版社，2004
（中国之光）
ISBN 7-119-03540-1

I. 新… II. 福… III. 福尔克纳，A.－回忆录－英文
IV. K836.124.2
中国版本图书馆 CIP 数据核字（2003）第 109630 号

外文出版社网址：
　http://www.flp.com.cn
外文出版社电子信箱：
　info@flp.com.cn
　sales@flp.com.cn

中国之光丛书

新中国：朋友还是敌人？

作　　者　（新西兰）福尔克纳（Falconer, A.）
责任编辑　蔚文英
封面设计　蔡　荣
印刷监制　冯　浩
出版发行　外文出版社
社　　址　北京市百万庄大街 24 号　　　邮政编码　100037
电　　话　(010) 68996121 / 68996117（编辑部）
　　　　　(010) 68329514 / 68327211（推广发行部）
印　　刷　三河市汇鑫印务有限公司
开　　本　小 16 开
印　　数　1000 册
版　　次　2004 年第 1 版第 1 次印刷
装　　别　精装
书　　号　ISBN 7-119-03540-1 / Z·700（外）
定　　价　48.00 元